TO SURVIVE CAREGIVING

A Daughter's Experience,
A Doctor's Advice,
On Finding Hope, Help, and Health

Cheryl E. Woodson, MD, FACP, AGSF
Family Caregiver, Geriatrician

Meryl L. Junious, Editor

ISBN 0-7414-3725-2

Published by:

PUBLISHING.COM

1094 New DeHaven Street, Suite 100
West Conshohocken, PA 19428-2713
Info@buybooksontheweb.com
www.buybooksontheweb.com
Toll-free (877) BUY BOOK
Local Phone (610) 941-9999
Fax (610) 941-9959

Printed in the United States of America

Printed on Recycled Paper

Published February 2007

TABLE OF CONTENTS

ACKNOWLEDGMENTS

This book is dedicated to my Heavenly Father, my Rock, my Sword and my Shield.

AND to the people who made this book possible:

- My parents, the late Arthur C. and Beatrice Woodson, were the wind beneath my wings.

- My BU (basic unit), my husband, Myron Murff, my son and daughter, Ryan and Lauren, and our pets, Leo and Keiya, keep me going.

- My big brother, Unca Docta Drexie, Drexel G. Woodson, PhD, I love you more than you know.

- My sister-in-law, certified genius, MacArthur Fellow, Brackette F. Williams, PhD, went upside my head to make me find the confidence.

- My Philadelphia family anchors me, especially my Seenie-Neenie (oops) Neenie-Seenie, my first mentor and MY angel smile child.

- The late Rev. Dr. Leon H. Sullivan and the congregation of Zion Baptist Church in Philadelphia, PA created an environment where excellence and intelligence were cool.

- So many church families nurtured me over the years, especially my current home with Pastor Mike Russell and his wife, Debbie, at Jubilee Faith Community, ELCA.

- My fifth grade teacher, the late Miss Anna Jean Cooper, demanded my best.

- My sixth grade teacher, Miss Josephine Polizzi, reminded me that I love to write.

- The late Earl D. Hanson, PhD lent me his strength when I wanted to quit.

- Gertrude Hughes, PhD gave me the tool of written language.

- Marcia Ontell, PhD and Marty Ontell, PhD caught me when I stumbled.

- David Satcher, MD, MPH saved my career by helping me reorder my priorities.

- Bennett Lorber, MD modeled compassion, humanity and excellence.

- David Solomon, MD modeled integrity, elegance and excellence.

- Thomas Yoshikawa, MD modeled tenacity, loyalty and excellence; he repeatedly passed me the ball and he gave me another commandment: *"Let not thine activities stray from the company of thine experience."*

- Joanne Schwartzberg, MD and Hugh Schwartzberg, JD always believed.

- The late Bernice Neugarten, PhD assured me I had something to say and her daughter, Dail Neugarten, PhD helped me focus.

- James R. Webster, Jr., MD always had my back.

- Patti Tighe, MD helped me find and heal the hurts.

- The geriatric social workers, nurses and care managers: Nina Brown, RN; Jennifer Cleary, RN, MSN, GNP; Allison Diemer, BSW; Ann Duncan, MS, RN; Marsha Foley, RN, MBA; Charlene Siegler, MS, RN, GNP; Ann Katz, MSW; Darby Morhardt, LCSW, ACSW; June Ninnemann, LCSW; Helene Raedle, LCSW, ACSW; Shelly Sachs LCSW, ACSW; Beth A. Sack, BA; and Kitty Watson, BS, MPA taught me how to play on the geriatrics team.

- The neurobehavior specialists: Kathy Aikens, PhD; Mary Avellone, PhD; Thomas Bartuska, MD; Leslie Blake, MD; Jeffrey Cummings, MD; Preston Harley, PhD; David Hopkins, PhD; the late Bob Lerner, MD; Stephanie Livingstone, PhD; Daniel Luchins, MD; Tim McManus, PsyD; Neil "the Snake" Pliskin, PhD; and Sandy Wientraub, PhD make it possible for me to do my job.

- The "Sistagirl" geriatricians' presence on the planet comforts me. I appreciate Sharon Brangman, MD; Jan Clarke MD, MPH; Cynthia Henderson, MD, MPH; Risa Lavizzo-Mourey, MD, MBA; Rita Lewis-Perry, MD; Toni Miles, MD, PHD; Veronica Scott, MD, MPH and especially Margaret Griffin MD, MPH and Adrienne Mims, MD, MPH who helped me get my stuff straight with honesty and love.

- Celia Berdes, PhD; Laurie Broadus, MLS; Micki Iris, PhD; Joanne Lynn, MD; Shai Hoffman, MA; and Diane Slezak, MBA helped me with the research.

- In this crazy kind of world, I'm glad I got my Girls: my cuz Deborah Brown, Minister Sharon Carey (aka Adair), Doris Mitchell Green, Sandy Guydon, JD, Mrs. Linda Hamer, Norweeta Milburn, PhD, my angel Caroline Nocho (aka Chubbie), Ms. Marie Palmer, Jeannette E. South-Paul, MD, Col., MC (RET) (aka Bess) and the past, present and future staff of Woodson Center for Adult HealthCare, SC who just -----stand.

- Master Patti S. Barnum and my American Taekwondo Association family at "Da 'Wood" lift me up.

- I am grateful to my meticulous editor, Professor Meryl L. Junious. Any errors reflect my impatience, not her professionalism.

- Some people were sharp instruments in the Hand of God; He used you to strengthen me.

- Most of all, this book is dedicated to my patients and their caregivers. You take better care of me than I ever take of you.

INTRODUCTION

If you are responsible for **any** care given to a person who cannot meet **all** of his or her own needs, you are a caregiver. Whether you live across the room, across town, or across the country, whether you give hands-on care, or you organize and supervise, you are a caregiver and this book is for you. The book is designed to give you permission to take care of yourself and it will show you how to do that while giving the best possible care.

You have your hands full!

I have seen families crushed by caregiving responsibilities in my twenty years of practicing geriatric medicine. Many of you care for parents, in-laws and other older relatives while you raise children and grandchildren at the same time. All of this is happening while you try to have a marriage, a job and a life!

You struggle to get doctors to tell you what your loved one needs now and in the future. You're mostly in the dark about the help that's available in your communities. You toil under the weight of guilt trips laid on you by people who don't like what you're doing, but won't step up to help you. It's not fair and it's not necessary.

You're taking care of them and killing yourself.

You're doing everything. You make sure your seniors have all the recommended tests and you see that they get to their doctor appointments on time. You get their prescriptions filled and you make sure they take every medicine in the right dose, at the right time. You make sure the house is in good repair. You make sure they eat the right foods in the right amounts according to their doctors' recommendations. You see that their bills are paid and their money is used wisely,

BUT how well do you take care of your loved one's most valuable asset? How well do you take care of **YOU**? What about **your** doctor appointments and prescriptions? What about **your** finances and family? You're so busy giving care that it's hard to step back to look at what **you** need. You have to put yourself closer to the top of your **"TO DO"** list.

Support should not equal suicide.

Caregiving should not make you sick. It should not mean the death of your career, your marriage, or other relationships. You should not have to sacrifice your finances, or your joy.

I've been there. I have practiced Geriatric Medicine for more than twenty years. For almost half of that time, I supervised the care of my mother as she lived and died with Alzheimer's disease. I had a family and a job just like you do.

I've also learned a lot from successful caregivers. I've seen how information, communication and planning can make it easier to carry the load. In this book, I'll share what I've learned from caregiving and from caregivers.

This book isn't about the folks you care for; this one's for you.

Although this book is focused on eldercare and many of the caregiver stories involve memory loss, the strategies I recommend will apply to all caregivers, regardless of the age of the person they care for, or the illness their loved one suffers. You can find help here whether you care for a sick child, a disabled adult, or a senior.

I won't give you a checklist of tasks to do. I won't tell you how to dress wounds, perform treatments, or give medicines. I won't try to explain Medicare Part D, or prescription drug expenses; that discussion would take over the book!

I will tell you how to get doctors to help you. I'll teach you how to communicate with doctors so they really listen. You can get doctors to tell you what your senior needs now and in the future. You can also arrange for doctors and other eldercare experts to stand with you, or in front of you, when other family members give you a hard time.

What if there aren't any other family members? Whether you're the only child, or the only child who's doing anything, there are practical solutions to help you.

I'll teach you how to explore the eldercare resources in your community. I'll also suggest ways to communicate with your seniors to encourage them to cooperate, but this book isn't really about your seniors. This one's for **YOU**.

Who looks out for you? Who cares how you feel?

You're a better caregiver when you develop a support team. In the game of football, the quarterback is the coordinator of the team on the field, executing the plays, reacting to new situations and organizing team activity. The linemen block the opposition and protect the quarterback. You have to be the quarterback of the caregiving team, not a lineman. You shouldn't try to do everything yourself.

How you feel doesn't have to dictate what you do. You can admit caregiving is overwhelming; you can even say you're sick and tired of caregiving, and **still give great care.** Sometimes, we caregivers are our own worst enemies. When **you** are the problem, you can learn how to move out of the way without losing control of the care plan.

I'm here for you.

You can lean on my experience as you deal with difficult and painful issues like family conflict, nursing home placement, end-of-life care and grieving. I want to share my experience as both Doctor Woodson and Daughter Woodson to affirm your feelings, to confirm your decisions and to comfort you.

I also hope to give you a smile or a chuckle to lighten your load along the way.

These stories are about real caregivers.

I hope you will see something of yourself in the real caregiver stories that introduce each discussion. Some of the stories are composites, but they all are real family situations from my own caregiving, or from caregivers in my medical practice. Identifying details have been changed to maintain privacy.

Use this book the way you need to.

Read straight through, or explore specific topics as they come up in the course of your caregiving. Either read the family stories and decide whether you identify with their struggles, or skip ahead to the discussions.

If you're not interested in public policy, you may want to skip the first and last chapters, but I hope you won't. Hands-on caregivers are the best advocates for seniors and other caregivers. These chapters will give you the ammunition you need to communicate with legislators, encouraging them to make eldercare policy more helpful for caregivers and for all Americans who live with chronic illness.

Instead of using the cumbersome phrases "she or he," "hers or his," "her or him" at every turn, when the discussion does not involve a specific person, I will alternate gender references.

Airline flight attendants tell us to put our masks on **first** when there are problems as we travel with people who depend on us. Take care of yourself, so you will be able to survive, thrive and even inspire others who struggle with the challenges you have right now. Taking care of you **IS** taking care of them. Read on.

CHAPTER 1: THE CRISIS IN CAREGIVING

Today's caregivers often feel guilty when they admit caregiving is overwhelming. Older relatives often say, "I don't see what you're complaining about. We always took care of everybody ourselves. Our family doesn't put people in nursing homes, or hire strangers."

The truth is, past generations of caregivers had nowhere near the responsibility today's caregivers face and they did not have to give care for such a long time. Today's caregivers are responsible for **more** older adults, **older** older adults and **sicker** older adults compared to caregivers in previous generations. Unfortunately, in the current generation, caregiver resources are shrinking; there are fewer caregivers to share the load. This is the Crisis in Caregiving.

Aging America: *More* Older Adults

According to census data, between the years 1900 and 2000, the number of Americans over age 65 increased 11 times over. In the same hundred years, the total population only tripled. The first of the babyboomers will reach age 65 in 2011. They will cause the aging population to double, from about 35 million to over 70 million seniors, in just 20 years. (1)

While sociologists may argue about the end of the "Babyboom," most agree that it began at the end of World War II. At each stage of life, babyboomers were the largest group in American history. They were the largest group of babies, children, teenagers and college students. When the first of the babyboomers reached age 60 in January 2006, they opened the door to the largest group of senior citizens our nation has ever seen. The Honorable Dorcas R. Hardy made this very powerful statement as Chairperson of the 2005 White House Conference on Aging:

"On January 1, 2006, the first of the babyboomers, born in 1946, will turn 60 and a 60th birthday for a boomer will continue to occur every 7.7 seconds for a LONG time." (2)

The Older You Get, The Older You Get: *Older* Older Adults

A woman born in 1941 was expected to live about 67 years.(3)Today, that woman is 65 years old and now, her life expectancy has increased about 17 years, to age 82.(4) If she reaches age 80, her chance of living to 100 is even greater than anyone would have predicted at age 65. At each stage, you have a greater chance of reaching the next age milestone, because you outlive accidents, infections, heart disease and other conditions that would have killed you. The oldest Americans (over age 85) quadrupled their number in the 20th century; their ranks are expected to grow another 5 times over in the next 50 years. (5)

Have We Gained Time, Or Are We Doing Time? *Sicker* Older Adults

To live long, you have to avoid dying. In the early part of the 20th century, the major cause of death was infection (6) and when people got sick, they either recovered completely or they died. In the past 70 years, medical advances have brought life-saving power. Antibiotics, blood transfusion, cancer chemotherapy and other powerful medications, artificial respiration (ventilators), feeding tubes, kidney dialysis, cardiopulmonary resuscitation (CPR), organ transplants and procedures that open, or bypass blocked blood vessels--- all of these medical miracles prolong life. Unfortunately, the time gained is not always good time.

While we benefit from technology that prevents death, we may live long enough to experience a painfully slow decline from heart failure, cancer, lung failure and complications of being inactive after a stroke.(7) For example, instead of dying suddenly from a heart attack, many people survive with weak hearts that get weaker every year. Their hearts pump less than 1/3 of the blood that a healthy heart pumps and they have so little energy they are seriously challenged to eat and breathe at the same time.

Doing More with Less: *Shrinking* Caregiver Resources

The need for care increased when the causes of death shifted from short-term, acute illnesses to years of suffering from chronic diseases. Caregivers are responsible for **more** older adults, **older** older adults and **sicker** older adults who need more care for a longer time. Unfortunately, there are fewer caregivers; they live farther away and they have many other life responsibilities in addition to caregiving. The imbalance between care need and care resources is the **Crisis in Caregiving**.

The following story depicts five generations of women who give and receive care in a typical American family. I intend no sexism; I do not mean to overlook male seniors, or the husbands, sons and other male relatives who give care. However, about 60 % of frail older persons are women (8) and about 70 % of caregivers are women. (9) By tradition and still by majority,

CAREGIVER = UNPAID, FEMALE RELATIVE.

Five Generations of Caregiving in an American Family

When GRANDMOM needed care, she had eight living children, four of whom were daughters. None of the daughters worked outside of the home during Grandmom's illness and no one lived more than five miles away from her. Grandmom lived with her second youngest daughter. The household also included three adult grandchildren and two great-grandchildren. When Grandmom needed care, her youngest grandchild was almost thirty years old. Grandmom's illness lasted about a month before she died of "old age" (probably pneumonia related to stroke).

MOM was Grandmom's primary caregiver. When she needed care for herself, Mom had six children, four of whom were daughters. Mom's primary caregiver, a daughter, lived in the same house as she did, along with another adult child and two teenaged grandchildren. Three other adult children lived within walking distance and the sixth child lived about 3 miles away. During Mom's illness, her youngest grandchild was eleven years old.

Mom's primary caregiver worked part-time. Another daughter was a full-time homemaker who lived around the corner. The other two daughters worked full-time outside of their homes, but neither of them worked more than forty hours per week. Mom's illness lasted about four months before she died of pancreatic cancer. Mom cooked Easter dinner for the extended family on the afternoon of the day she died.

MOTHER was one of Mom's daughters. She was not as lucky as Grandmom and Mom were. Mother had only two children and only one was a daughter. Mother lived with Alzheimer's disease for about ten years. For much of Mother's illness, her caregiver lived more than five hundred miles away.

The caregiver worked more than sixty hours per week in a professional career while raising two children. Mother's youngest grandchild was two years old when her care needs began; the grandchildren were nine and thirteen years old at the time of Mother's death.

DAUGHTER is not any luckier than Mother was. She has two children and she gave birth to her only daughter at age thirty-nine. If Daughter should become ill at the same age Mother did, GRANDDAUGHTER may not have finished her education, or she could be in the early stages of developing her career. If Granddaughter has children by then, they could be even younger than Daughter's children were during Mother's illness.

****

Each generation supports a larger number of older adults who need more care for a longer time. There are fewer caregivers and they live farther away from their seniors. These caregivers also have other responsibilities that compete for their time and energy.

Early in Mother's illness, Daughter also assisted in the care of her mother-in-law. Caregivers may have responsibility for parents, grandparents, in-laws, aunts, uncles and other older loved ones all at the same time!

Many mid-life adults find themselves responsible for children as well as seniors. Substance abuse, incarceration, mental illness, unemployment, divorce and parental abandonment leave many children essentially orphaned. Grandparents are standing in the gap. The number of adults with primary responsibility for grandchildren (or other relatives' children) increased by almost 30% between 1990 and 2000. (10)

A fifty year-old caregiver may support two seventy year-olds, a ninety year-old and teenage, or school-aged children, while trying to work, plan for retirement and stay married. This has to change.

CHAPTER 2: GET HELP FROM PROFESSIONALS

Don't Deny; Don't Delay; Don't Despair.

The most important steps toward getting help are to:

- Recognize that your loved one has a problem.

- Move quickly and confidently to get the resources you need.

Two barriers to recognition are denial and agism.

****

Don't Deny: D'Nile Is Not Just a River; Stay Out of Egypt.

Mrs. M lived alone for twenty years after her husband's death. She was very active in her church and community and she had a wide circle of friends. Her children lived in another state, but they called weekly and either she visited them, or they came to see her several times each year.

Mrs. M had been a snappy dresser, but over the past year, she attended church in clothes that were soiled and in clashing colors. She missed functions by showing up a day early, or a week late. She volunteered to label food baskets for the poor, but she could not follow the directions for how to fill the baskets. Her baskets were always missing several items, or she put in too many of the same things.

Mrs. M never seemed to have any money. She always told friends she left her wallet at home. The friends paid for several trips and meals, but Mrs. M never repaid them. In the past, she had always been eager to split costs fairly. After one outing, Mrs. M pulled out of the church parking lot without looking and she almost hit a car. She turned in the wrong direction; she had to be flagged down and turned around before she could get home. Mrs. M's friends began to pick her up to take her to functions.

One evening, friends came to take Mrs. M to a church concert. As they prepared to leave her home, a young man rang the bell. Mrs. M immediately went into her purse and gave him ten dollars. When questioned, she laughed, saying it was the man's birthday. She told her friends she always gave "the kids a buck or two."

One of the friends called Mrs. M's son to voice her concern. Mr. M Jr. said, "Mom's just being generous. She was upset by almost having an accident and she just got a little turned around. Making mistakes with the baskets is no big deal. She was probably just tired."

Several weeks later, the church friends were turned away from the door by the young man they had seen earlier. They heard loud music and they saw several other young adults in the living room. When they returned with the police, they found Mrs. M alone and crying with bruises on her face and arms. There was no food in her refrigerator and the freezer was empty. Her television and VCR were gone. Her purse had been emptied onto the floor and the cash and credit cards were missing.

Mrs. M went to stay with one of her friends. When her son came to town, he found **stacks of unpaid bills, an empty bank account and $30,000 dollars in credit card debt.**

****

According to folklore, ostriches bury their heads in the sand thinking they are safe, because they cannot see the danger. We can imagine that the birds are in denial; **ostriches get their backsides shot off all the time.** If you put your head in the sand, you actually present a bigger target and the outcome can be much worse. If Mr. M Jr. had intervened as soon as he heard there was a problem, he might have kept his mother from harm and he might have protected her income.

He did not want to see that she had a problem. So, he did **nothing.**

Maggie Kuhn-Founder of the Gray Panthers

Agism can also cause denial. Agism is a bias against older adults, but it is also the expectation that older adults should be disabled. Many of us believe that any problem an older adult experiences is caused by "just getting old." We lower our expectations for their health and their behavior.

****

Mrs. F is a 75 year- old woman who is very active in her local drama and dance troupe. Over the past year, she has noticed increasing knee pain that interferes with her dancing. Mrs. F and her family and friends thought that slowing down was to be expected at her age. After a few months, Mrs. F stopped driving to performances and she turned down rides from her friends. Her family assumed Mrs. F was tired and needed "more rest at her age." Soon, Mrs. F withdrew from all social activities. She spent more time alone, sitting in front of the TV. When her family visited, they noticed that Mrs. F seemed surprised to see them even though they had called to tell her they were coming. Mrs. F's previously pristine housekeeping and fastidious personal care were lacking. Her family assumed she was "just getting senile."

Mrs. F called 911 because of sudden chest pain and shortness of breath. A blood clot developed in her leg because of inactivity and the clot had traveled to her lungs. After a week in the hospital on blood thinners, Mrs. F was too weak to go home alone. She was transferred to a rehabilitation facility and her family began to look for a nursing home.

The rehabilitation specialists made the diagnosis of depression. Mrs. F received psychotherapy and anti-depressant medication while physical therapists worked to strengthen her knee. She returned home with an exercise program to keep her knee strong. Mrs. F's memory, mobility, spirit and her life returned to normal. She is dancing again.

****

If either Mrs. F or her family had understood her decline was not related to aging, she could have participated in physical therapy before the pain made her stop dancing. Immobility triggered a cascade of problems that could have caused permanent disability, or death.

Despite the media blitz for products that promise to make us more youthful, aging is not optional. The body does change with age, but most of the changes reflect a lesser ability to handle stress, or injury. Older adults react to stress more severely and they recover from injury more slowly than younger adults do. At rest, or when there is no illness, or other stressor, older adults can perform as well as younger adults do, though they may not perform as quickly.

Dementia is a devastating disease of progressive brain failure that steals memory and independence. Many people believe all older adults have dementia, but in truth, only about 5% of Americans between age 65 and 75, suffer from dementia; 95% of them **don't** have dementia! This illness is more common with aging. In people over age 85, about 50% of people suffer from dementia ;(11) 50% of these seniors **don't** have dementia! If an older adult shows a sudden change in memory, or behavior, the change may be caused by a medication, an infection, or another reversible problem.

Maggie Kuhn, founder of the Gray Panthers insisted, "**Age is *not* a disease!**" Don't give up and accept disability without a thorough investigation. Older adults are not supposed to be confused, suffer pain, leak urine, fall, lose interest in life, or change in any other significant way unless there is an illness. It's not just that they are getting old; they may have a condition that could be improved, if not cured. Even when we can't cure, we can give the right care. Don't deny that there may be a problem. Don't be agist and assume the problems you see are "just old age."

The Mayo Clinic Website [12] lists five warning signs to alert caregivers that an older adult may be at risk:

- Weight loss
- Change in ability, or interest in housekeeping, gardening, cooking, card playing, or any other activity where the senior used to excel
- Change in personal appearance and hygiene
- Increased sadness and social withdrawal
- Problems with mobility

I would add another warning sign. Be suspicious if a senior begins to mismanage money. Does he pay bills on time? Does she forget to pay bills? Does he spend large amounts of money on strange purchases? For example, one senior bought $25,000 worth of electric beds. Another previously astute businessman bought $12,000 worth of packing materials, but he failed to pay his quarterly business taxes.

Don't Delay: Dare to be Direct.

If there is even a hint of a problem, investigate immediately. Some illnesses can be improved, or even cured. When you delay, you may let the damage continue until the opportunity to cure is lost. An investigation can confirm your worst fear; the condition may not be curable, but if you delay, you may miss a chance to ease suffering.

Families are often reluctant to impose on an elder, to offend, or interfere, but here's the important question: **Would you rather have an angry mother, or a safe mother?** (See Chapter 6: Balance Independence and Safety)

****

Mr. R's family was increasingly concerned about his driving; he often drove 20 miles per hour in a 55 mile per hour zone. He frequently straddled the yellow line and he needed to be reminded to turn at familiar corners. The family did not want to "limit Dad's independence." They argued, "He only drives in the neighborhood and to his sister's house."

One Sunday afternoon, Mr. R's sister called his son to report that Mr. R had never arrived for dinner. There was no answer at Mr. R's home and no one had heard from him. The pastor reported that no one had seen Mr. R after church.

The family searched the neighborhood frantically and at 9pm, Mr. R's son received a call from the police in a town over 200 miles away. A large water pipe ruptured on the street Mr. R usually traveled between church and his sister's house. Barriers were erected to direct drivers to a detour, but when he turned off the familiar road, Mr. R could not remember how to get back on track. He drove until he ran out of gas. Then, he walked away from his car and he became increasingly agitated and confused. The police found him wandering down the interstate highway. Mr. R was lucky not to have been mugged or hit by a car.

****

Mr. R was endangered by his family's decision not to "offend him," but how does a family know when to intervene, or what to do? Professionals help families find answers.

Don't Despair: There *Is* Help.

Help is available through comprehensive geriatric assessment that tells families how much care their loved one needs. Geriatric care managers help families find resources that allow them to put the recommended care plan into place. When families have this information, they can avoid giving too much care and wearing themselves out, or giving too little care and committing elder abuse and neglect.

****

Mrs. McG was 101 years old. Her memory was sharp, but she needed a cane because of arthritis in her knees. She lived with her 83 and 85 year- old daughters who were healthy and active. The three ladies functioned as a team, sharing meals, chores and household expenses.

One morning, when one of the daughters went to wake her mother, she noticed Mrs. McG's face was twisted and her speech was garbled. The right side of Mrs. McG's body was paralyzed and the daughter had to call her sister to help get their mother out of bed. The daughters called 911 and Mrs. McG was admitted to the hospital with a stroke.

Mrs. McG's condition improved very little while she was in the hospital. The daughters decided to bring their mother home with support from a home health agency and a home care physician instead of admitting her to a nursing home.

The doctor visited two weeks after Mrs. McG's discharge from the hospital and found that her daughters were exhausted. They were working hard to see that that none of their mother's needs were neglected, but they were not attending to their own needs. They changed Mrs. McG's bed linens four or five times every day. They made hearty soups for all of her meals and they gave her a different soup for each meal. The soups were made from scratch, using fresh vegetables and meats that one of the daughters bought each day from a farmers market 15 miles away. Between the laundry, shopping, cooking and other household chores, both daughters were in danger of wearing out. If the daughters became ill, all three of the ladies could end up in a nursing home.

The doctor worked with the home care nurse and social worker to give Mrs. McG a comprehensive geriatric assessment. The team found that Mrs. McG could follow commands. She could also point to letters, words and pictures on a board to make her needs known. She could transfer from her bed to a chair with the assistance of one person. The nurse ordered a bedside commode and the physical therapist taught the daughters how to move their mother safely. By taking Mrs. McG to the bathroom frequently, the daughters decreased their laundry load considerably. Everyone convinced the daughters that Mrs. McG could eat the same food they ate if they mashed fruits and vegetables and used a blender for meats.

The social worker arranged for a homemaker from the community care program to help with the housework. The helper also stayed with Mrs. McG for a few hours each day so the daughters could rest and resume some of their social activities. This care situation remained stable until Mrs. McG died quietly at home 6 months later.

****

Comprehensive Geriatric Assessment

The geriatric assessment goes beyond the basic medical examination to also evaluate memory, communication and other brain functions, vision, hearing, mobility and nutrition. The geriatric assessment team also reviews medications to insure that they are "gero-friendly." This means the medications are prescribed in appropriate doses for an older adult's system. The medication review also looks for side effects and interactions between medications, whether they are prescribed or purchased over-the-counter. It also looks for interactions between medicines, vitamins and other nutritional supplements.

Comprehensive geriatric assessment answers five essential questions:

- What is wrong with Dad?
- Why is it wrong?
- How much can be fixed?

- How do we fix what we can?

- How do we manage the part that's not fixable?

The goal of the geriatric assessment is to investigate a senior's ability to remain independent.

Geriatric assessment teams include a geriatrician, a doctor who is trained in internal medicine (health care for adults), or family practice. Then, the doctor spends at least one additional year of specialized training in the care of older adults. After completing this training, the geriatrician takes an examination to earn subspecialty board certification in Geriatric Medicine. This credential is jointly conferred by the American Board of Internal Medicine and the American Academy of Family Physicians. The credential must be updated by re-examination every ten years.

In an effort to attract babyboomers (many of whom insist on designer labels), some doctors add "geriatrics" or "gerontology" to their business cards and other advertising. This is intended to show they are "designer doctors" for seniors. BEWARE! **Gerontology** is the **study** of aging; a gerontologist studies and conducts research about aging. **Geriatrics** is the **practice** of providing health care and services to older adults; a geriatrician is a doctor who takes care of older adults. Do not be deceived. The terms "gerontologist" and "geriatrician" are not interchangeable. A doctor can be both or either, but a doctor who takes care of patients full-time and advertises as a gerontologist is probably **neither**.

Other members of the geriatrics team may be nurses, social workers, nutritionists and pharmacists, as well as behavioral health and professionals in Physiatry (physical medicine and rehabilitation). Geriatric assessment can last several hours on one day when all members of the team are located in one place. There are also "virtual teams" with members who function in a community network, working in different offices. Then, the assessment usually occurs in 60 or 90 minute sessions over two to three weeks.

Regardless of the length of the assessment sessions, caregivers will want to make the most of the time to be sure that all of their loved one's needs are addressed. Several essential strategies increase the likelihood that the doctor will listen to all concerns and answer all questions:

- Give complete information. The geriatrics team will need to know what problems the family sees. The team will need specific examples of tasks the older adult can perform well and a description of the activities that are difficult for her.

- Someone must accompany the senior to the geriatric assessment appointment. The family member who has the most contact with the older adult is more important than the one who happens to be available to provide transportation that day. Of course schedules and other commitments must be considered, but the person who has the most useful information should at least send a list of medications, concerns, comments and questions.

- Even if the primary resource person is present, a written list of questions will keep concerns in focus and insure that all questions are addressed during the visit. It may be useful for the primary caregiver to bring another advocate who can provide an extra set of ears and another opportunity to understand information. However, office space may not accommodate several relatives in the initial interview.

- Ask for written instructions to review after the visit. Ask about procedures to follow if questions arise later. Ask about the protocol for relaying messages to the doctor and getting responses. These answers will avoid telephone tag and improve the flow of information. (See Chapter 2: Physician User's Manual)

Tests are usually ordered to confirm or clarify any problems found during the first visit. The tests may include blood samples and x- rays. More intensive testing may be ordered by specialists when specific body systems may be at risk. These systems may include the heart, lungs, kidneys, brain, digestive tract, muscles, joints, hormones and other organ systems. Geriatric assessment may also include information from surgeons and professionals who specialize in brain function. Once all of the information is gathered and reviewed, the team usually convenes a family conference to give recommendations and answer questions. (See Chapter 2: Family Conference)

How Do You Find A Geriatrician?

Several community resources can help caregivers locate a qualified geriatric assessment program. Many university hospitals and medical schools offer training programs in geriatrics. Information may be available from local area agencies on aging, state medical societies, local geriatrics societies, physician referral telephone lines, home health agencies and hospice programs. The American Association of Retired Persons (AARP), the American Geriatrics Society and the American Medical Association are all good resources for finding a geriatrician, or a geriatrics team. (See Resources)

You may be able to find a geriatrics team through human resource departments, employee assistance programs, lawyers, bankers, realtors and other professionals who serve an older adult clientele. This is especially true in communities where the eldercare network is strong and well coordinated.

Many older adults resist evaluation, because they are offended that their adult children think they need help. The seniors may feel less threatened if a healthy spouse, a friend, or an adult child asks the senior to join him in "getting a check up." A reluctant older adult may also agree to a comprehensive geriatric assessment if a trusted primary care physician (PCP or family doctor) recommends the assessment. This referral extends the mantle of trust and credibility from the PCP to the geriatrics team. If the PCP says, "I need some information from a specialist," the geriatric assessment is a consultation and the geriatrician is seen as working with the PCP.

Families can also take the senior out for a meal, or other activity and just end up at the geriatric assessment site. Professionals in geriatrics programs are trained to diffuse tension and to dispel resistance. We can often turn resentment into curiosity, or at least grudging cooperation with the geriatric assessment team. I often thank a senior for giving me the opportunity to evaluate "a healthy older adult," or when I am working with medical students, I ask the older adult to "help me teach young doctors the proper respect for older people." Often, this puts the geriatric assessment in a more positive light.

Level of Care Prescription

The level of care prescription is the most valuable product of a geriatric assessment. This recommendation is developed after the team learns how the senior functions. Can the older adult perform all of the tasks necessary to remain independent? If there is a difference between what the older adult needs to do and what she can do, this **is** the level of care.

The geriatric assessment team develops the level of care prescription to tell caregivers:

- What type of care is needed
- How often the senior needs care, how many hours he needs in each care session and
- How much training, or education the caregiver should have

Will it be enough if the grandson brings groceries and helps with finances once a week, or should the caregivers be registered nurses who can bandage wounds and administer complex medications 24 hours a day?

The **level** of care (what your loved one needs) and the **locus** of care (where the care can be provided) are separate decisions. Someone who needs 24-hour supervision may not need a nursing home if there is enough family support, or if the person can afford to hire in-home help. If the person can walk, if she does not need complex medical procedures and if she has enough money, she may be able to live in an assisted-living facility instead of a nursing home.

The locus of care depends on the level of care prescription, the resources available in a given community and family finances. The level of care prescription comes from a doctor. Caregivers are best guided through the locus of care decision by social service professionals, geriatric social workers, or geriatric care managers.

Geriatric Care Managers

These professionals are usually social workers, or nurses whose input is invaluable at any stage of geriatric assessment. Geriatric care managers are excellent resources for finding geriatricians, but they can also make home visits to start the evaluation process for seniors who refuse to see doctors.

Geriatric assessment teams prescribe the level of care and geriatric care managers help families develop the resources to put the prescription into place. Geriatric care managers save caregivers time by narrowing the list of options according to what is appropriate for the level of care, for patient and family values, and for family finances. These professionals can cut red tape by weeding out inappropriate resources and by helping to prepare applications for services. Geriatric care managers are very skilled in addressing issues in family relationships that can undermine care plans. They are also outstanding in caregiver counseling, education and support.

The National Association of Professional Geriatric Care Managers website (www.caremanager.org) provides lists of certified geriatric care managers by zip code. Many state-funded social service agencies have case management units that serve the same function as the private geriatric care managers. The cost of these services can range from fees calculated on a sliding scale based on income, to rates that usually start at about $75 per hour. Geriatric care management fees can exceed $200 per hour, but these hours are in care coordination, not in hands-on care. After the initial assessment, the care manager may only spend a few hours monitoring and updating the plan. Some long-term care insurance policies cover care management services, but these services are not covered by Medicare, or other health insurance programs.

Regardless of the finances, many families find that hiring a geriatric care manager is the best money they ever spent. Care managers ease caregiver stress, because caregivers are less frustrated as they find care services. They also get support and peace of mind.

Family Conference: Professionals at Work, Don't Try This at Home

The level of care prescription is one product of comprehensive geriatric assessment and the family conference is the other one. Family conferences support caregivers and help them arrange excellent care for older adults. Unfortunately, family conferences can deteriorate into shouting matches that berate already overwhelmed caregivers and fail the older adult. The conflict often leaves deep scars on family relationships that continue to cause pain long after the senior dies.

Care conferences are most productive when families find common ground in the love they feel for the senior and in their desire to give the best care. Families need an objective referee who has enough credibility to help move conflicts aside, while helping everyone focus on where they agree. I do not believe a family member can serve in this role.

In my experience, the family is in turmoil because the one who holds that respected position is the one who needs care. If Grandma were healthy, she would issue marching orders and everyone would fall in line. Things fall apart, because Grandma cannot use her influence to stabilize the situation.

The facilitator should be a professional who is experienced in the illnesses of aging, eldercare resources and family dynamics. A geriatrician, a geriatric social worker, geriatric care manager, or a nurse practitioner usually serves in this role, but psychiatrists, psychologists and clergy are also very effective facilitators.

The facilitator keeps individual family members out of the line of fire. This specialist keeps the lid on counter-productive emotions and controls blame-laying, or name-calling. The expert learns about family values, provides education, reviews resources and outlines reasonable care options. The facilitator also takes the heat for introducing difficult topics such as nursing home placement, limits on independent functions like driving, or end- of-life care.

Every family member who is interested in the care plan should be invited to the conference. I often include out-of-town relatives in a conference call with a speakerphone; everyone has an opportunity to express concerns. This strategy eliminates the "he said, she said' that leads to misinformation and misunderstandings, because everyone hears the information at the same time.

The family conference also supports the caregiver. Since the information comes directly from the expert through the level of care prescription, the caregiver's requests for help have more power. She can say, "The doctor says Mom needs this." The geriatric expert **prescribes** the plan of action; the baby sister does not tell the other siblings what to do. Family members lose the right to criticize the caregiver when they either fail to respond, or fail to follow through on the help they promise. (See Chapter 3: Show up or Shut Up)

Darby Morhardt is a social worker at Northwestern University Medical School and she is a master at helping families develop and implement plans of action.

****

Darby and I served as co-facilitators for a very large and volatile family. The primary caregiver was the youngest sister and she was worn out. Everyone else disagreed with her about nursing home placement for their grandmother; they insisted that the family would care for Grandmom.

Darby asked whether the family members wanted two, three, or four-hour shifts throughout a 24 hour period. She asked, "Who will take 8am to noon, noon to 4pm…." and she made a chart that covered shifts around the clock. Darby documented the shift each family member agreed to and she made copies of the schedule for everyone. Family members agreed to cover a shift, run errands, assume other responsibilities, or contribute funds to hire a respite worker for a shift.

Everyone agreed to review the plan in one month, but by the second week, several shifts had gone uncovered. Family members didn't show up, or they cancelled at the last minute. They balked when the primary caregiver asked them to pick up groceries, or take her children to school. No one came up with any money. The primary caregiver had to take unpaid leave from work and she dipped into her own pocket to hire workers to fill in the gaps. Nursing home placement was arranged and no one had anything else to say. (See Chapter 3: Show Up or Shut Up)

****

This caregiver gained information and support from the geriatric assessment and the care manager. The caregiver learned what needed to be done; she put a plan into place and her final decisions were supported by the information and actions of the geriatrics professionals.

New Era of House Calls

The practice of physician home visits is increasing after a long hiatus. (13) The American Academy of Home Care Physicians has a membership of over 1,000 doctors. Several medical companies provide physician services solely in the home. Home physicians can perform geriatric assessments and provide ongoing primary care. Home health agencies, area agencies on aging, state and city departments on aging and medical societies are good sources of information about physicians who make home visits.

Adult Day Care, Community Eldercare Services, Assisted-Living Facilities and Respite Care

Departments on aging, area agencies on aging and local eldercare agencies offer a variety of services for which the costs are based on income. Private agencies offer the same range of services, including housekeeping and laundry, meal preparation, bill payment, shopping, chore services, transportation and personal care. Some private services also help families find appropriate housing for seniors based on the level of care prescription (See: Resources). Private services are usually more expensive than those offered by state-funded programs, but they may be more accessible. In some states, there may be a long waiting list for state-supported services.

Adult day care programs provide supervision, social interaction and activities, bathing, meals and medications. These programs help working caregivers, but the services are valuable for any caregiver who needs a break during the day. Many adult day care centers offer transportation services and some programs offer evening hours.

Assisted-living and supportive care facilities offer housekeeping, meals, activities and limited supervision. People who need nursing care are not usually eligible for these facilities, but medication and personal care services may be available at extra cost.(See Chapter 10: The Myth of Assisted-Living)

Respite services are designed to give caregivers intermittent breaks. Respite workers can come into the home for a few hours each week, or they can stay over a weekend. Seniors can stay in assisted-living facilities or nursing homes to provide respite when a caregiver needs a longer time for an emergency, a surgical procedure, a vacation, or any other absence.

REMEMBER! Geriatric care managers help families contact agencies, establish eligibility and complete application forms to access community eldercare resources. These professionals also provide initial assessment, caregiver counseling and support.

Physician User's Manual: Getting the Most From Your Doctor

Caregivers are often frustrated as they try to get information from doctors, but there are effective ways to get the help you need from physicians.

****

Mr. G's family was so angry with Dr. H. Daughter #1 sat in Mr. G's hospital room all day, but she never saw the doctor. She asked the nurses to page Dr. H, but he was examining another patient and he could not come to the phone. The nurse left a message for Dr. H to call Mr. G's "daughter" and she was told that the doctor would call at the end of the day. Mr. G usually comes to the office with Daughter #2, so Dr. H called Daughter #2 at 8pm to review the care plan with her. Daughter #2 had not been to the hospital and she had not spoken to her sister. She was not aware of her sister's concerns and she could not ask the necessary questions.

The nurses told Daughter #1 that Dr. H usually made rounds around 7am. She informed the hospital security guard she was there to meet with the doctor and she came up to the floor at 6:45am. Dr. H came at 7:30, but he had six more patients to see in the hospital before starting his office hours at 9am; he did not get a chance to answer all of her questions. Daughter #1 was livid. "That doctor made me come in here for nothing. He breezed through here a half hour late and he didn't even give me the time of day. He's not the only one who's busy; I have to work, too."

****

Communicate By Appointment, Not By Ambush

Would you stand outside of a courthouse and try to talk to your lawyer as she rushed in to represent another client? Would you walk in to a beauty salon and ask the stylist to stop working on the client in the chair to work on your hair?

No! In either instance, you would make an appointment, because if you did just show up, you would not get the service you needed. It's the same with your doctor.

Most doctors have several practice sites. We make rounds at one or more hospitals each day; we see patients in the office and in several long-term care facilities. Some of us also make home visits. We see many patients at each site. Time is tightly scheduled and even if you can "catch" the doctor on rounds, the doctor has scheduled this time to care for the patients in that facility. The doctor will rarely be able to stop right then to give you the amount of time you need.

The same is true when you ask a nurse to page the doctor while you are in the facility, or when you call the office and expect the doctor to come to the phone immediately. If your mother had an appointment in the office, would you want the doctor to leave her in the examination room to have a non-emergency conference with another family? Have the same consideration for the person in the doctor's office when you put in a page, or call to "see how Grandpa's doing."

Can Someone Else Help You?

When you call the doctor's office, be specific about what you need and be willing to talk to nurses, medical assistants, managers, or other members of the doctor's support team. Some caregivers refuse to tell the receptionist what they need because of privacy issues, or because they don't respect the essential role of support staff in a good medical practice. In most practices, the office staff functions under protocols that are specifically designed by the doctor. These protocols direct the staff to prioritize and respond according to the type of question and the level of urgency. The staff cannot help you effectively if they do not know what you need.

Tell The Staff What You Need: Be Specific!

"I need to talk to the doctor" is not an effective message. The office staff follows specific instructions about which calls are serious enough that the doctor will leave an examination room to answer them immediately. Otherwise, the staff follows protocol to:

- Direct patients with emergency medical problems to the emergency department, or

- Schedule patients with urgent medical problems into special office appointments, or

- Relay the doctor's orders about tests to guide treatment decisions

Patients commonly call the doctor's office about medical problems and medications, test results, requests for prescriptions, referrals, or forms. Many calls also involve billing information and copies of medical records. You can usually get answers more quickly if you route these questions through the receptionist, nurse, or office manager.

The general "I want to talk to the doctor" calls are usually returned at the end of the day, after the doctor has seen all of the patients in the office and after she has handled every urgent call. If there are many urgent calls, the general calls could be bumped to the next day. The support team needs to know what you need so they can help the doctor respond appropriately. Be sure to leave all of your contact information: daytime, evening and cell phone numbers. A growing number of practices communicate by e-mail. Ask whether this is an option and get clear instructions about any e-mail conference fees. Most insurance plans do not cover conferences by telephone, or e-mail. You may be asked to pay for these interactions.

Getting Doctors to Give You the Time You Need

Emergencies are the nature of medical practice. No one can tell you exactly when the doctor will return your call, but you should be able to get a time frame-- morning, afternoon, evening, within 24, or 48 hours.

The best way to get the time you need with the doctor is to schedule a conference. You can meet with the doctor in the hospital, or in the nursing facility, but be prepared to meet in the doctor's office. Please do not bring several family members to a routine, 10 or 15 minute office visit, expecting an impromptu conference. Other patients have appointments, too; the doctor will not be able to give you enough time. You must schedule conference time in advance.

Make the appointment through the doctor's office staff. Hospital, nursing home and assisted-living personnel do not usually have access to a schedule that shows all of the doctor's activities.

Medicare and other health insurances usually cover the cost of a conference if the older adult receives medical attention on the same visit and if he participates in the discussion. A senior who is very ill may not be able to participate in the conference. When seniors are confused or agitated, their presence can actually interfere with the care planning process. This is especially true if there is family discord, when the seniors are upset by shouting, or worried by the general "negative vibe" in the room. In the ideal situation, the physician will have the patient's prior permission to speak with the family, or a family member will have the legal right to make decisions (medical power of attorney).

When the older adult cannot be at the conference, the family should be prepared to pay a conference fee. Ask about the fee when you make the appointment.

Concerned family members may miss the conference because of conflicting work schedules, or because they are far away. I use the conference call format with a speakerphone when this is an issue. No travel time is involved and every interested family member can participate. Working family members can attend the conference during a scheduled break.

Sometimes, conflicting schedules make meetings impossible even with a conference call. Some families do not want to work together, but family members have to talk to each other! It is unrealistic to expect the doctor to talk to everyone individually and it is usually impossible for the doctor to schedule several conferences. The family must agree on a "point person" to communicate with the doctor and relay information to everyone else.

The Health Information Privacy and Accountability Act (HIPAA) makes it impossible for the doctor to give information to just anyone who calls with a concern about the senior, no matter how sincere that person is. The only people who may receive medical information are those with written permission from the patient, a medical power of attorney, or legal guardianship.

A family member who is not the legal advocate may still have vital information to contribute. For example, when the doctor is looking into Mom's "unexplained falls," it would be important for a family member to share that Mom drinks two six-packs of beer every night. It is always best when this information is funneled through the point person, but in some families, strained relationships make this impossible.

HIPAA says, as a doctor, I cannot talk to an unauthorized person. **HIPAA does *not* say this person can't talk to me.** Write a note, send e-mail, or a fax to communicate any information you want the doctor to review. The doctor cannot respond to you without written permission from your senior, but the information can have great impact on your loved one's care.

During the first office visit, it is my policy to ask **every patient** for permission to speak with an advocate, regardless of the patient's age. I encourage patients to prepare powers of attorney, but I also ask them to make and sign a list of the people they want to have access to their health information. Patients prepare the list and they state the order in which I should call potential advocates. I get the information before there is a crisis and permission is available when I need it. This strategy also avoids arguments with family members; if your loved one did not put your name on the list, **I cannot talk to you.** Take it up with your loved one.

You should schedule a conference if your doctor either:

- Passes off all problems as "just old age"
- Never contacts the point person to discuss the care plan
- Fails to relay information through staff, or
- Otherwise refuses to communicate.

You can also send a letter to discuss your concerns. If you are still dissatisfied, request a consultation with a geriatrician. If these strategies fail, think about looking for a new doctor. Today, medicine is a customer service industry. You can get good service and you deserve it. Just realize, as with any other service, you should expect to pay for it.

To survive caregiving, you must get the help you need from professionals. You have to accept that the problems exist (don't deny), move quickly to learn what you have to do (don't delay) and feel confident that there is help to find the resources you need (don't despair). Your survival kit includes comprehensive geriatric assessment, the level of care prescription and effective communication with physicians, geriatric care managers and community eldercare resources. These professionals can help you find services and they can provide ongoing education and support.

CHAPTER 3: GET HELP FROM FAMILY AND FRIENDS

When we are lucky, caregiving can bring families together with strong communication and common goals. Unfortunately, caregiving can also open rifts, reveal grudges and air unspoken conflicts. Some caregivers trudge on, thinking they are doing what is best, when their methods actually make caregiving harder. Caregivers can recruit support more effectively.

Don't Ask, Don't Tell---Won't Work: Let People Know You Need Help.

Some families keep illness a secret to protect a loved one's reputation. This leads to disaster.

****

The Reverend Dr. P was the backbone of his family and for over fifty years, he was the well-loved and respected senior pastor of a large church. Over a three- year period, Pastor P's wife noticed that his behavior became increasingly strange. He took off his shirt and he asked church members to rub lotion on his back. He repeated the same sermon several times in one month. One day, Pastor P went out to visit a parishioner, but Mrs. P found him sitting in the car in front of the house twenty minutes later. He could not remember how to start the car. Pastor burned food, left dishtowels on top of the stove and amassed $10,000 in debt to telemarketers.

Mrs. P became increasingly reluctant to leave Pastor alone at home. Mrs. P could not quit her job at a local florist, because she carried the couple's supplemental health insurance and prescription plan. She also truly enjoyed creating flower arrangements. Rev. and Mrs. P had several adult children who lived out of town. They also had a large network of friends, but Mrs. P thought Pastor would be embarrassed if anyone knew he needed help.

Initially, Mrs. P called to check on Pastor several times each day, but when he stopped answering the telephone, she began to drive home at lunchtime. One day, she sped through a red traffic light. She was involved in a car accident that dislocated her shoulder, bruised her knee and her hip.

Mrs. P's injury alerted the rest of the family and it prompted everyone to look for other options. Pastor P's primary care physician referred him to a geriatrician who made the diagnosis of dementia (progressive brain failure that steals memory and function). After Pastor's medical evaluation, a meeting was held with Mrs. P, her children and the elders of the church. They decided to give Pastor a party to honor his career, to celebrate his retirement and to usher him into the role of Pastor Emeritus. Several retired friends and deacons rotated the responsibility of "visiting" Pastor, taking him to lunch and "accompanying" him on visits to the sick and shut-in. As Pastor's condition declined, Mrs. P's children worked with her to finance adult daycare and to investigate future care resources.

****

Disability is not a character flaw and it should not be hidden from other family members, neighbors, church members, or business associates. You need all the help you can get; everyone's eyes, ears, hands and ideas will be useful. Maintaining an illusion to protect a reputation can endanger lives: the senior's, the caregiver's and sometimes, as in the case of a fire or a dangerous driver, hidden disability can endanger society at large.

Take the "S" Off Your Chest, or Step Away From the Kryptonite: You Can't Do It Alone.

Caregivers try to do the impossible. They don't accept that it **is** impossible until a change in their own health interferes with the caregiving.

****

Mr. S described himself as an "independent, tough old coot." He had smoked three packs of cigarettes every day since his teens. He also struggled with high blood pressure and high cholesterol. Mr. S developed emphysema and memory loss related to many tiny strokes. He was unable to manage his housekeeping, because he was short of breath; he could not manage his finances because his memory and judgment were poor. Mr. S's daughter, C, worked the night shift and she had two school-aged children. Her husband worked as a consultant in a position that required out of town travel at least two weeks every month.

Daughter C spent her days helping her father in his home across town and her nights at work; she got very little sleep. As her children grew and became involved in activities outside of school, the situation became unmanageable. Mr. S argued, but eventually, he agreed to move into Daughter C's home.

Daughter C thought this move would be good for everyone, because Mr. S would not have to spend money on housing and he could help take care of his grandchildren. Unfortunately, Daughter C's son had asthma and Mr. S did not want to limit his smoking to the back porch. The move to a less familiar environment made Mr. S's confusion more obvious and the active children agitated him.

The next year, Daughter C discovered she was pregnant. Mr. S's memory and function had declined so severely that he needed 24-hour supervision. Daughter C was reluctant to leave her father alone with the children, because of Mr. S's agitation and loud outbursts. In the second trimester of her pregnancy, Daughter C began to have contractions and she noted spots of blood in her underwear. Her doctor ordered bed rest for the duration of the pregnancy.

Daughter C and her husband realized this was the last straw. Her husband accepted a management position that required less travel. Daughter C submitted a request to return to her company in a day position after maternity leave and Mr. S moved into an assisted-living facility designed for people with memory loss.

****

It was a bit much for Daughter C to work full-time at night and care for children and a dependent adult during the day, without the daily support of her husband. This fact never occurred to Daughter C. She did not have a realistic view of the number of straws on her camel's back until she was faced with the possibility of losing her baby.

Caregivers often fail to realize they have taken on too much. Many caregivers accept the whole responsibility without question and they feel guilty if they buckle under the strain. I ask these caregivers, "if someone told you the story you just told me, would you be surprised they were having trouble coping?" The universal answer is "no;" yet caregivers can't seem to give themselves the same compassion they would give others. Caregivers believe they are SUPERCAREGIVER! Unfortunately, they stumble into Kryptonite, usually in the form of an illness, or another condition that saps the last of their strength.

"Ye Have Not Because Ye Ask Not:" You Have To Ask.

Some caregivers are reluctant to ask for help. Others believe they should not have to ask and they are bitter when family members do not offer to help spontaneously, but "ye have not because ye ask not."(14)

****

Mr. and Mrs. B have been married for 60 years and he became a full-time caregiver when she suffered a stroke. Before the stroke, the Bs had an active life in community service. At first, Mr. B tried to take his wife everywhere with him, but she couldn't walk well and she tired easily. Mr. B took care of the house and yard, the car, the finances, the laundry and the cooking. After several months, he became fatigued and less involved in activities he enjoyed. Since he no longer played cards, or went bowling with his buddies, Mr. B became isolated.

Both Mr. and Mrs. B had siblings who visited regularly, but Mr. B was angry that the siblings did not offer to "help more." He admitted he had never asked for help directly. His sisters thought Mr. B "seemed to have everything under control." Mr. B finally admitted he needed more time to himself. He asked one of his sisters to spend a few hours a week with Mrs. B, so he could have lunch with his buddies. Sister was happy to help out.

****

Don't assume people know what you need. Don't expect them to read your mind, or to recognize needs that are obvious to you. They may think you have everything together; they can't help if you don't let them know you need help.

Be specific. "Why don't you give me more help with Mom" is too vague. Once a geriatrician prescribes the level of care the best way to communicate the need is to say, "the doctor says Dad needs A, B and C. I've done A, can you do B, or C by next Thursday (or another specific time)? This language is precise. It also shows that you have accepted a role; you are not just dumping on the other family members. It gives the family member a choice of tasks and specific language gives everyone a time frame to manage.

Show Up, or Shut Up: If They Don't Help, They Can't Criticize.

Influential and assertive family members may have strong opinions about the care plan and they often voice their disapproval in no uncertain terms. Caregivers may act on these opinions even though the recommendations are unrealistic, when no help is offered, or when help is promised, but it does not materialize.

****

Mrs. K was a tireless community advocate until she developed heart failure. Arthritis in her spine damaged the nerves in her back and caused pain when she tried to move her legs, but she was too weak to undergo surgery to correct the condition. Mrs. K fell several times and she had a minor car accident when she could not move her foot from the gas pedal to the brake quickly enough. Eventually, Mrs. K became short of breath with any movement and walking was impossible. Mrs. K forgot to pay bills and she got lost driving to the senior center where she ate lunch everyday. It was clear that she could no longer live alone in her third-floor, walk-up apartment.

Mrs. K had three children, but only her youngest daughter, N, visited regularly. Daughter N took her mother to the doctor and she assisted with medications. She did her mother's laundry, housekeeping and grocery shopping. Daughter N also worked full- time and she took night classes in a master's degree program.

Daughter N looked at options as her mother's health deteriorated. She and Mrs. K considered an assisted-living facility, or moving Mrs. K to a first-floor apartment with hired help in the home.

Mrs. K had several sisters in the same community. They thought Daughter N should stop working, move into her mother's home and use her own funds to pay for a chairlift for Mrs. K. The sisters were quite vocal in their opinions that

Daughter N owed this to her mother, their sister, but none of them offered to help with chores or errands. They visited Mrs. K only at their convenience. They did not offer to take her to their homes, or on outings and no one offered any financial support.

Daughter N wanted to be respectful to her aunts and she tried to juggle her schedule and her finances to care for her mother. Within a year, Daughter N became exhausted and she could not continue. After joining a caregiver support group, Daughter N moved her mother to a first-floor apartment; she used Mrs. K's money to hire part-time caregivers and she arranged daily transportation for her mom to the senior center. Her aunts kept complaining and Daughter N kept taking care of her mother and herself.

****

Commitment + Accountability = Entitlement

Sometimes, family members offer to help and fail to follow through, but they still feel entitled to comment on the care plan.

****

Mr. O'M developed heart failure and liver disease after years of hard drinking. His legs were swollen; he walked slowly and he often forgot to take his medicine. He lived in his home with Daughter E, who worked nights in a bakery. Son A was a successful lawyer who lived downtown. Mr. O'M chose Son A to have power of attorney for health care and finance, because of his son's profession and his status as the eldest child. There were no other family members.

Daughter E gave Mr. O'M his medicine, prepared meals, cleaned the house and did laundry before going to bed at about 2 pm. She left for work around 10:30 pm after bathing her dad and putting him to bed. Mr. O'M woke his daughter several times each evening and he called her frequently through the night, complaining that someone was in the house. Sleep interruptions left Daughter E exhausted; the phone calls caused problems with her employer.

Federal Express delivered packages to the house every day. The packages contained merchandise from television shopping programs, but Mr. O'M denied placing any orders. He also hid the packages. Mr. O'M became angry when his daughter asked him for a permanent marker to make return labels. He could not understand what she wanted even though he had used markers to label packages in a shipping department for over thirty years. Return shipping was costly; Daughter E often found the packages too late to return them for refunds. She worried about finances; she worried about leaving her dad alone and she worried about keeping her job.

Daughter E needed to curb Mr. O'M's spending; she needed to rest, to work without interruptions and to relax with friends. She asked her brother to help by calling their dad in the evenings and taking him out for a few hours on the weekends. Son A agreed wholeheartedly, but every time his sister asked for a specific time, he gave her a list of his many time commitments. Son A saw no reason to cancel Mr. O'M's credit cards, to use his dad's money to hire help, or to arrange adult day care.

A neighbor agreed to help Daughter E by sitting with Mr. O'M for a few hours three evenings a week and every other weekend. One winter night, the neighbor called Daughter E at work. Mr. O'M had come to the neighbor's door at midnight, wearing only his pajamas, without a coat or shoes. The neighbor could not convince Mr. O'M to come into her house, so she walked him home. Daughter E left work early; the bakery manager was not pleased.

Daughter E tried to convince her brother that their dad needed help, but Son A made light of all of her concerns. "Why shouldn't Dad buy whatever he wants and why should he recognize a permanent marker after all these years?" Son A was not concerned about Mr. O'M's midnight trek in the snow. "He just needed to stretch his legs." Son A accused Daughter E of being too eager to restrict Mr. O'M's independence; he also said his sister was selfish and ungrateful. "You left Dad with a stranger after all he's done for us!"

Daughter E was angry and heartbroken. She had always looked up to her brother and she did not want to fight with him. She wanted to take care of their dad, but she could not continue under the current conditions. She gave her brother several options. He could either:

- take more responsibility for their dad's direct care, or

- respect Daughter E's concerns about their dad's needs, giving full emotional and financial support, or

- give up his power of attorney and agree not to contest his sister's petition for guardianship of Mr. O'M

Daughter E decided to move out and leave her brother with both **responsibility and authority,** if he did not get with the program.

Son A was shocked into action by his sister's ultimatum. He agreed to a comprehensive geriatric assessment for Mr. O'M and he worked with his sister to put the level of care prescription into action. They protected their dad's money; they hired workers for evenings and weekends and they arranged respite care for vacations.

****

No matter how much caregivers love and respect them, family members lose the right to criticize when they offer no help, or when they offer help and fail to follow through. Caregivers do not have to actually tell anyone to show up or shut up. Just inform family members about the level of care the doctor prescribed; ask them for help and hold them all accountable for the help they offer. Remember the conversation I suggested in Chapter 2: Getting Help From Family and Friends. "The doctor says Mom needs A, B and C. I've done A. Can you do B, or C by D time?" When relatives do not come through with the help they offer, the caregiver should do what she needs to do. She can remind relatives of their broken commitments when they criticize, or she can just ignore them and get the job done in a way that works best for her and the senior.

Do not accept responsibility without authority.

Daughter E was Mr. O'M's primary caregiver, while Son A had the right to make all of the financial and health care decisions. This is unfair. The person with direct caregiving responsibility cannot have her hands tied as she tries to provide the care. Frontline caregivers must have a major role in deciding how to use financial resources for care. If the caregiver is not the guardian, or legal power of attorney, the person who has that authority must support the caregiver completely.

If You Don't Want to Drive All the Time, Take Your Hands Off the Steering Wheel: Let People Help You.

Sometimes caregivers berate others for not helping when actually, they undermine all efforts to help.

****

Recall Mr. B whose sister agreed to stay with Mrs. B while he had fun with friends. Sister relieved Mr. B one Saturday afternoon, but when Mr. B returned, he was irritated that Sister made turkey sandwiches for lunch instead of tuna. She and Mrs. B folded laundry instead of watching television. Mr. B was sure Mrs. B had been upset by all of this and he insisted, "she called for me the whole time." Since that

Saturday, Sister has come for short visits, but she hasn't offered any more help.

****

Caregivers often insist "no one can do it as well as I can." (How did Mr. B know whether or not Mrs. B cried for him all afternoon? He wasn't there!) If you really want help, you have to let people help. Don't tell them how to do something unless a specific diet, medication, or treatment is prescribed by your loved one's doctor. Of course, you should tell helpers about routines and preferences, but don't hover or criticize. Do tell them if a specific activity is particularly effective, but does it really matter whether he wears the blue shirt, or the green one? Be generous with your praise and appreciation. You catch more flies with honey.....

Sometimes caregivers refuse help, because emotionally, they are not ready to lose the older adult. Subconsciously, they may believe they can prevent further disability, or death by controlling every aspect of care. I have worked with many families where one person made all other activities and relationships secondary to the caregiving role. These caregivers either consciously insisted on caregiving alone, or subconsciously, they made sure no one else had the opportunity to give care.

These caregivers need the most support. They can fall into deep depression when the older adult's condition deteriorates despite their best efforts. These caregivers are at high emotional risk when the older adult dies. One caregiver said she no longer knew who she was; she wasn't sure she had anything to live for after her caregiving role ended.

Get used to getting help early in the caregiving process. Don't wait until you're too exhausted to go on. Make arrangements for the help to come regularly, so you can always look forward to time for yourself. Then, you can step back and remember who you are, what you enjoy and how to enjoy it. (in Chapter 4, See: Find Joy Outside of Caregiving)

CHAPTER 4: PROTECT THE PRIMARY RESOURCE—Hey, That's YOU!

You take care of your seniors' medications, money and housing. You try to protect their dignity and keep them happy, but do you protect the single resource that makes everything else possible? How well do you take care of **You?** Caregivers suffer more depression, chronic illness and early death than people of the same age who are not giving care.[15,16,17] Caregivers reduce work hours, or they make other changes in work schedules that put their incomes at risk. They retire early, or they deplete financial resources that would bring comfort to their own senior years. [18,19] It makes good sense to invest in the physical, financial, emotional and spiritual health of your loved one's most valuable resource—**YOU!**

Physical Health: Avoid Your Loved One's Fate

You probably know exactly when Mom will take her last pill and you call to refill her prescription in plenty of time. Dad's doctor appointments are etched in your brain, but have you refilled your medication? When was your last appointment? It is impossible to give good care if you neglect yourself. If something happens to you, what will become of your loved one?

****

Mr. J is 67 years old and he cares for his 87 year-old mother, Mrs. O'L, who suffers from heart failure. Although her mind is clear, she is confined to a chair and she needs help to transfer from the bed, the toilet and the bath. Mr. J retired three years early to care for Mrs. O'L and he struggles to make ends meet on a smaller pension than he expected. His brother and sister-in-law live in another state. They call often and they visit when they can, but there is no other family.

Since Mr. J stopped working, he has gained about 40 pounds. His knees hurt, he has much less energy and he no longer plays handball with his buddies. His job was in a smoke -free environment and he used to smoke only a few cigarettes each day. Now that Mr. J is retired, he smokes all day, consuming a pack and a half of cigarettes every day.

Before his retirement, Mr. J was active in his local Masonic lodge and he was one of the best bowlers on his bowling team. He went to baseball and basketball games, movies and other social gatherings with friends. Now, Mr. J leaves his mom only to buy groceries and gas. He never goes out with his buddies and after years of being turned down, they don't call much anymore.

Every night, after he puts his mom to bed, Mr. J does laundry, cleans the house, pays bills and cooks for the next day. Mr. J sleeps poorly. He stays up into the wee hours of the morning, watching videos and drinking at least a six-pack of beer every night. Mr. J tries to convince himself he isn't lonely.

Mr. J's last physical examination was just before he retired. His doctor warned him that his cholesterol was high and he was at risk for developing diabetes. Mr. J continued to take medication until his refills ran out. He spent his time taking Mrs. O'L to her doctor appointments, helping her with personal care and physical therapy exercises, entertaining her, cooking and keeping house. Mr. J never had time to go back to the doctor for treatment, preventive care, or prescription refills.

For the past few months, Mr. J has felt slightly nauseated and short of breath with any activity. At first, these symptoms occurred only when he brought groceries up the stairs, but for the past week, the symptoms have occurred even at rest. Mr. J took the trash out to the curb early one morning, because he had been too tired to take it out the night before. Suddenly, he felt hot; his left arm ached and it was hard for him to breathe. He turned to go back into the house, but he collapsed on the sidewalk. An hour later, his neighbors came out to go to work and they saw him lying on the ground. They called an ambulance, but it was too late. Mr. J was pronounced dead from a heart attack when the ambulance arrived at the emergency room. Mrs. O'L was admitted to a nursing home.

****

Your older loved one is likely to die before you do, but you *can* die first, leaving your senior behind. Who will take care of your loved one, then? Even if Mr. J had not died, he could have ended up in a nursing home along with his mother. Is that what you want? If not, you should take better care of your health.

In chapter one, we saw that Americans are living **longer**. The key to living **better** is protecting your health in the earlier adult years. **At age 50, you're planning for age 80.** Invest in your health now, so you can live the way you want to live in your golden years.

The following discussion is not intended as an exhaustive exploration of preventive health strategies, nor is it intended to replace your doctor's advice. The most important step toward protecting your physical health is to find a primary care doctor to advise and work with you. Your doctor will help you implement these recommendations as they apply to you. I have chosen to highlight topics that raise the most questions among caregivers and other patients in my medical practice.

Heart Health

Heart disease is the number one killer of Americans.[20] It is also the most common cause of death among women over age 40; this is the group that contains most of the caregivers.[21]

You did not pick your parents. You cannot change the genes you may have inherited for an increased risk of heart disease, but genes are only a blueprint for what **can** happen. Lifestyle often determines what does happen, when it happens, or whether it happens or not.

Strategies for protecting your heart include not smoking, controlling your weight to decrease your risk of diabetes, and managing your cholesterol and blood pressure.

Do Not Smoke!

Smoking contributes to the top four diseases that kill Americans: heart disease, cancer, stroke and chronic lung disease.[22] Even if smoking does not kill you, it is a risk factor for many conditions that cause slow deterioration. Instead of killing you quickly, these conditions can make you wish you were dead. Smoking can lead to emphysema and heart failure---illnesses that can make it a challenge to perform even simple activities while you try to breathe at the same time. Can you imagine having to choose whether to breathe or to eat?

Smoking contributes to stomach ulcers, osteoporosis and poor circulation that can cause painful leg infections and amputations. There may also be problems with sexual performance. Smoking allows these conditions to kill your independence and quality of life before they actually kill you.[23]

If you want to have all of the good years you can, stop smoking now! It is never too late to stop, but smoking can be a very difficult addiction to conquer. Your doctor can help. Medicines, hypnosis, acupuncture and other techniques are available to help you stop smoking. Talk to your doctor now.

Get Fit and Stay Fit!

Maintain a Healthy Weight

Extra weight makes your heart and lungs work harder. Being overweight is a risk factor for diabetes, high cholesterol, high blood pressure, heart disease and arthritis. You didn't put the weight on over night, so don't expect to lose it overnight. A weight loss of one or two pounds per week is perfectly reasonable. You need to take in 500 fewer calories each day if you want to loose one pound per week. Three cans of a non-diet soft drink, two chocolate candy bars, or two cans of beer all contain about 500 calories. Small changes can have a big impact. If you lose one pound per week, you'll lose about 50 pounds in a year!

Most sensible eating plans recommend a diet that is low in fat, low in starch, high in fiber and higher in protein. It is also recommended that most people should consume about 64 ounces of water each day, but you should ask your doctor how much water is safe for you. Safe eating plans also recommend that you eat small meals more frequently to avoid long periods of fasting. Fasting forces the body to slow its metabolism to store energy; the storage form of energy is fat. **Eat early and eat often!** You would not start your car without gas, so why would you start your day without breakfast? Try to eat three smaller-portion meals and three healthy snacks each day, each spaced about four hours apart. Eat smaller portions more frequently, decrease fat and starch, choose low fat sources of protein and load up on veggies, fiber and water; then you can be successful in losing weight safely.[24]

Are You Feeding Your Stomach or Your Mind?

Food is only an energy source just as are coal, gas and wood, but many of us have psychological issues we address by eating.[25,26] Food becomes love, comfort and stress management. Many people find the strength to overcome emotional eating in a support group, or with personal counseling.

People who have had difficulty losing weight over many years should work with behavioral health counselors, while they follow plans for healthy eating and exercise. Some people blame excess weight for their life circumstances and they are sure these circumstances will improve when they lose weight. People's lives do improve with weight loss, but I believe these people feel better about themselves once they are more fit and their **behavior** changes. These people may have more energy; they may be more open to new experiences and new ideas. They may have more confidence about making life changes. It is the change in **behavior** that changes their circumstances, not just the change in their **weight**.

Psychologist, author and television personality, Dr. Phil McGraw asks, "How's it working for you?"[27] Does your current approach to weight loss meet your goals? Does the current plan make you happy?

I believe there is another way to interpret Dr. Phil's question. You may see food as comfort, not just as energy, or the extra weight may serve some purpose you may not recognize. You may not be aware that you want to protect the unrecognized benefit of being overweight more than you want to be healthy (See: the story about Mrs. A in the following section on weight loss surgery). Under these conditions, you can sabotage yourself and fail to meet your weight loss goals. Counseling can help you understand what food means to you. Counseling can help you recognize how the extra pounds are not "working for you," so you can develop more healthy coping strategies and find success in fitness. Find a program that works for you and drop the extra weight. Your doctor can help you decide how much weight you should lose and direct you to the program or eating plan that's best for you.

Get Moving!

A complete exercise program should include activities in the following fitness areas: "Cardio" or aerobics, resistance training, flexibility and balance. Exercise offers the added benefits of stress reduction and an opportunity to connect with other people. There are community exercise classes for every age and fitness level.

Aerobic exercise gets your heart pumping and it burns fat. Walk, bike, skate, invest in a treadmill, or a stationary bike. Recumbent bikes are great for people who have pain in the back, hips or knees. You should be able to talk during these activities, but you should be puffing a little and working up a sweat.

Your doctor, a certified personal trainer, or a physical therapist can help you decide on the best aerobics program and recommend the best equipment for you. They will also help you calculate the proper heart rate to maintain during exercise, based on your age and fitness level.

Resistance training builds and defines muscles and **Muscles=Metabolism.** If you increase your muscle mass, you lose weight more effectively; because you burn energy (food) more efficiently.

Ladies, don't be afraid of muscles. Your body doesn't make enough testosterone (male hormone) to turn your body into a mass of muscles that look like lumpy rocks. While it is not possible to "spot reduce," you will be surprised how effectively resistance training can sculpt your body. For example, when you add muscle to your shoulders, your hips may look smaller!

You can join a gym, or buy home equipment for resistance training, but you don't have to spend a lot of money. When it comes to exercise programs, you are not alone in backsliding. Other people have also bought pieces of exercise equipment, only to use them as clothes racks. Slightly used exercise equipment is often available over the

Internet, or in sporting-goods stores that sell second-hand merchandise. Exercise equipment may be more affordable than you think.

Exercise balls, resistance bands and hand weights are inexpensive. If you are significantly overweight, or if you are just starting an exercise program, your own body weight may provide enough resistance.

You can learn to use your muscles safely with exercise video tapes, DVDs and classes, but certified personal trainers are a great investment. Trainers challenge you to work hard enough to get results, while you decrease the risk of injury. The services of one trainer can be shared with two or three friends for a social connection, a support group and a cost-effective fitness plan.

You can locate a trainer in your area through recommendations from friends, neighbors, or co-workers who work with trainers, or by contacting fitness clubs. Sports Medicine programs, orthopedic surgeons and physical therapists may also have information on trainers. I cannot recommend a specific organization, but there are several reputable programs that certify personal trainers. One of these organizations, the National Strength and Conditioning Association, has a checklist of questions to ask potential trainers. (www.ncsa.org)

When added to exercises that increase muscle strength, **Flexibility and Balance training** can decrease the risk of injury from falls. Yoga, Pilates, T'ai Chi, Taekwondo and other martial arts combine cardio, resistance, flexibility and balance, while offering the additional benefits of stress reduction.

There is No Excuse!

Regardless of your physical limitation, there is an exercise program for you. Water exercise programs and swimming are great exercises for people who are extremely overweight, for people who are just starting to exercise, or for people who live with arthritis. You can even exercise while sitting in a chair.

You **do** have the time. You have every minute God gives you. The question is: how do you choose to use your time? You can carve out time for yourself when you develop a caregiving support team, make use of respite care, adult day care, or other services. **Just do something!** Any movement you enjoy will do, such as skating, dancing, martial arts, **ANYTHING!** You just have to move.

A Word of Caution About Short-cuts to Weight Loss

An exhaustive discussion of diet pills, colonics, severe fasting, fad diets and weight loss surgeries is beyond the scope of this book, but so many caregivers and other patients in my medical practice ask about these programs, I want to give a word of caution. Pills, surgery and other invasive procedures may cause rapid weight loss, but they may result in a rebound gain of even more pounds. Some of these agents may be dangerous and in my experience, the dangers are not always physical.

****

Mrs. A cared for her mother who suffered from Parkinson's disease. Mr. A supported his wife in caregiving, but he sought physical intimacy in relationships outside of their marriage. There were a few instances of infidelity early in the marriage, before Mrs. A became a caregiver. Even so, Mrs. A blamed Mr. A's behavior on the weight she gained in her caregiving years. At 5 feet, six inches tall, Mrs. A weighed over 300 pounds.

Mrs. A had been "chunky" in junior high school. Over the years, she tried several diets and numerous weight loss pills. She also purchased several pieces of exercise equipment that gathered dust in her basement. After years of disappointment with advertised "miracle" products, Mrs. A almost despaired of finding success, until she decided on gastric surgery.

Eighteen months after the procedure, Mrs. A was a svelte 150 pounds. She had more energy and greater self-esteem. She became more active in her community and she enlarged her circle of friends. Mrs. A set out to romance her husband, but Mr. A did not stop philandering.

Mrs. A had painted a romantic picture that surgery and weight loss would transform her marriage. Instead, she had to face the reality that her husband did not intend to be faithful. Mrs. A shed many tears saying, "I thought my life would change."

One day, Mrs. A stopped at a red light on her way home from the supermarket. A man stopped his car next to hers; he lowered his passenger side window and said, "Hey, Sugar, would you like to go for coffee?" Mrs. A raced through the red light, narrowly avoiding an accident. Minutes later, she sat in her driveway, breathing rapidly, sweating and in the throes of a full-blown panic attack. She was overwhelmed by the previously repressed memory of being molested by an uncle at age 13. Mrs. A had never told anyone, but that episode began her relationship with food as comfort and defense. Subconsciously, she had thought, "If I'm fat, men won't notice me. I'll be safe."

Mrs. A was devastated. She buckled under the pressure of disappointment in her marriage and she had to relive the shame, pain and loss of trust that comes with sexual abuse. She began to drink heavily and she started to regain the weight. Mrs. A was irritable with everyone; she was unable to care for her mother with as much love and patience as she had before.

A behavioral health counselor helped Mrs. A work through the real issues that contributed to her weight gain. She also developed other skills to cope with life stress. Mrs. A took advantage of a community care program that sent a respite care worker into her home for four hours every day. She used the free time to join an exercise program and a weight loss support group. Three months later, Mrs. A weighed about 150 pounds again; she also insisted that her husband either come into marriage counseling, or find another place to live.

****

After weight-loss surgery, your stomach area is about the size of your thumb and you are unable to eat the way you did before. Your weight and your risk of diabetes and heart disease should decrease, but you have the same job, the same marriage, the same family, the same financial problems and the same caregiving challenges. If the reasons for your weight gain are related to life stress, these reasons do not change with the surgery.

Several patients in my medical practice and several of my acquaintances use food to manage the stress of caregiving and other life challenges. Several of them have chosen to address their weight problems through surgery. Once their weight loss slowed and the novelty of rapid body changes passed, many of these people developed depression. Some of them turned to alcohol, gambling, excessive shopping, or high risk sexual behaviors. **If you don't strengthen the leg, when you remove the crutch, you will fall over.**

If you choose a surgical approach to weight loss, enroll in a program with a strong behavioral health component and participate in the aftercare program for as long as possible. This may help you avoid negative behaviors.

Safe, successful weight loss requires a change in lifestyle to include sensible eating and regular exercise. If you do not learn to understand your relationship with food and change your habits, then pills, colon cleansing, surgery and all of the other drastic measures will not help you maintain a healthy weight. Several of these agents can actually cause harm. Change your lifestyle and you can save the money you would have spent on pills, potions, severe programs and exercise equipment that you hate to use. Instead, you can treat yourself to something special like a vacation, spa services, or a snazzy, new wardrobe.

Prevent Cancer

Medical specialists develop guidelines about preventive cancer screening. These guidelines recommend the age at which screening should begin and they suggest how often screening should occur. These guidelines change as new information is developed by scientific study; so you should consult your doctor.[28]

Cancer Screening in Women

Women should ask about the current recommendations on breast examination and mammograms. They should also discuss Pap smears, pelvic examination and other specific tests to screen for cancer of the cervix, uterus and ovaries. Neither age nor hysterectomy dictates that a woman should **never** have another Pap smear. Your primary care physician or gynecologist can advise you on the appropriate screening intervals for you.

Prostate and Colon Cancer

Men should discuss the timing and frequency of prostate examination and blood tests for prostate specific antigen (PSA, a protein that can be elevated in disorders of the prostate including, but not limited to cancer). Everyone should learn about colon cancer screening with tests for blood in stool, or a colonoscopy (a lighted scope passed through the rectum to allow a specialist to look directly at the lining of the large intestine). If you have family members with colon cancer, if you or your family members have a history of polyps in the colon, or if you are over age 50, you should discuss routine colonoscopy with your doctor. If you notice a change in your bowel habits, or blood in your bowel movements, you should contact your doctor immediately.

Osteoporosis

Screening for osteoporosis involves a painless scan that measures bone mineral density. This test becomes important for women who are either over age 50, or more than 10 years past menopause. Women and men should ask their doctors about osteoporosis screening if they:

- Have broken a bone in the spine

- Smoke or drink heavily

- Use steroids or thyroid medicine

- Have conditions that affect the level of calcium in the blood.[29]

Immunize to Prevent Serious Infections!

Influenza and Pneumonia

Vaccination against influenza and pneumonia is recommended for people with diabetes, heart, lung, liver, or blood diseases and for everyone over age 65. People with cancer and people whose immune systems are suppressed either by cancer chemotherapy, steroids, or Human Immunodeficiency Virus (HIV) are also candidates for these vaccines. Even if you are not in a high risk group, caregivers should be immunized against influenza. You may not suffer severe consequences if you become ill, but you could transmit the disease to frail elders in your care, putting them at risk of death. The pneumonia vaccine is also recommended for people who have sickle cell disease and for anyone who does not have a spleen.

Tetanus

Tetanus infection is an uncommon, yet deadly illness. Tetanus is less than 50% curable, but it is almost 100% preventable. This disease can occur in unclean wounds. Most people associate tetanus infection with animal bites and stepping on a rusty nail, but the illness can also be contracted in pressure sores (bed sores), or by exposure to soil in gardening. In America, most cases of tetanus occur in older people with debilitating, chronic illnesses who have not been properly immunized. A booster every ten years just makes good sense.

Other Immunizations

Immunizations are available to protect against viruses that cause hepatitis (inflamed liver) and chicken pox. Chicken pox can be dangerous to children with chronic illnesses and to adults who were not exposed as children. This same virus can reactivate, causing shingles, a painful rash which can lead to blindness, or severe pain that lingers for years after the rash resolves. The need to immunize against these viruses and less common infections depends on your risk and on other conditions such as world travel. Talk to your doctor.[30]

Sexual and Urinary Function

Female Sexual Function

Changes in sexual function can significantly alter quality of life. Orgasm can be less intense and more difficult to achieve. Hormones like estrogen (the female hormone) and testosterone (the male hormone) have been used to improve orgasm. Unfortunately, both hormones have been associated with changes in cholesterol that may increase the risk of heart disease. Estrogen may also increase the risk of cancer of the female organs.[31] After menopause, the lack of estrogen can cause women to suffer vaginal dryness, painful intercourse and painful urination. Lubricants are useful and applying estrogen creams to the vaginal area can be beneficial. When used under the direction of a physician, local estrogen can be effective without causing side effects throughout the body. There are also behavioral techniques couples can learn to enhance sexual pleasure.

Erectile Dysfunction (ED)

A man's ability to sustain an erection depends on blood flow through the blood vessels in his penis. The conditions that cause poor blood flow to the brain, heart, kidney and legs can cause ED as well. High blood pressure and the medicines used to treat hypertension, smoking, diabetes and high cholesterol can all cause ED. Before a man begins any of the popular medications for ED, a doctor may decide to investigate the risks of other blood vessel diseases; ED medications can cause death in men who are also using nitrates, medications commonly prescribed to treat symptoms of blocked blood vessels in the heart. The treatment of ED is not limited to medications. A thorough discussion with a urologist is helpful in determining the best approach. (32)

Over Active Bladder (OAB)

Overactive bladder (incontinence or leakage of urine) can affect women and men, causing embarrassment and inconvenience. In women, incontinence can be caused by menopause. In men, disorders of the prostate can cause leakage of urine. Both sexes can be affected by bladder infections, or changes in the nerves that control bladder function. The commonly advertised incontinence medications can worsen some forms of OAB. Appropriate use must be guided by a thorough medical evaluation. Behavioral treatments include urinating on a regular schedule, limiting fluids within two hours of bedtime and avoiding caffeine which acts like a diuretic (water pill), increasing urine flow.(33)

Nutritional Supplements

There are a million vitamins, minerals and supplements; there are a million opinions about what is best. Safety dictates that you understand what supplements are appropriate to your medical condition. It is also important to consider how these agents might interact with the prescription medications, over-the-counter drugs and any other substances you use. Your doctor will recommend whether or not you should use aspirin to prevent heart attack and stroke. The doctor will also advise you about which vitamins, minerals and other supplements are right for you and in what amounts.

Get Enough Rest

I can hear you laughing, but sleep is important. When you are tired, your memory, judgment and organizational skills can be rusty.(34) **Also, you feel lousy!** Sleep deprivation contributes to car accidents and medication errors that could have disastrous consequences for your older adult; 1/3 of all hospital admissions in the elderly are caused by medication errors.(35)

Avoid using alcohol to help you get to sleep. While you may fall asleep more easily with alcohol, the sleep is more fragmented and less restful.(36) Over-the-counter or prescription sleep medications may cause you to feel hung over the next day, leaving lingering negative effects on function and judgment. Some of these agents may cause confusion, leakage of urine, falls, or problems in people who have glaucoma. Sleep medicines may also become addictive.

Establish a sleep routine (it worked when you were a baby; it will work for you now). Set a regular time to get up and a regular time to retire each day. It is also a good idea to have a nightly ritual such as a bubble bath, stretching, prayer, meditation, soft music, or light reading. The ritual slows you down and gives your body a signal that it is time to prepare for sleep. If you find you still cannot fall asleep, do not lie there and worry. Get up and do something relaxing, then try again. It also helps if you use your bed for sleeping and sexual activity, not for eating, working, or watching TV.(37)

If you are still sleepy when you wake up in the morning, if you nod off to sleep during the day and especially, if you are overweight and snore loudly, you may suffer from **obstructive sleep apnea**. In this condition, blood oxygen levels drop, making you wake up to breathe. These awakenings last only a few seconds, but they can occur hundreds of times each night, interrupting your sleep. Your doctor can order tests to confirm this. The treatment is simple and it can be life changing.

In Chapter 2, you learned principles to help you protect your loved one's health. You should apply these same principles to your own health care plan. **Don't Deny.** Many people avoid doctors and screening tests because they are afraid to discover something is wrong (We also discussed what happens to ostriches back in Chapter 2). If there is a problem, the problem is there whether you address it or not. **Don't Delay.** It's better to know about a problem early enough to keep it from destroying your health. Left unchecked, the problem will eventually get your attention with pain, bleeding, weight loss, or some other uncomfortable symptom. By then, it may be too late to avoid the bad outcome you feared. In fact, when you deny and delay, a negative outcome that was only a possibility can become very real.

Advances in medical science have allowed doctors to find potential illnesses early enough to prevent or cure them. Of course, some of us will get bad news. The earlier you know about a serious illness, the better you can intervene to either improve, or contain the condition. You can also put your affairs in order and make plans to soften the blow for you and your family. **Don't Despair.** See your doctor regularly to be sure you are doing everything you can to stay as healthy as you can.

Financial Health: The DOs and DON'Ts

Many caregivers bankrupt their present and their futures. They retire early, work fewer hours, or invest too much money in caregiving.(38) Other caregivers depend on seniors they care for to maintain their own financial stability. Both situations are dangerous and both situations require a clear understanding of the financial Dos and Don'ts of eldercare.

****

Mrs. F had two daughters, V and L. Daughter V lived in an apartment about 30 minutes away from Mrs. F. Daughter V worked full-time to support her two children and she maintained the usual expenses for her car and her household. She gave Mrs. F money to help with medicine, food and home maintenance. Daughter L had been unemployed for two years. She lived with Mrs. F as did her four children under the age of 10. Mrs. F did the cooking and she helped to care for the children.

Mrs. F suffered a stroke that affected her memory and partially paralyzed one leg. Walking had been difficult because Mrs. F already had poor circulation and arthritis. Now, walking was impossible. Mrs. F could no longer care for herself, or anyone else.

The daughters refused nursing home care when the doctor recommended it, because they didn't want to "leave Momma with strangers," but there was no other family to help them care for Mrs. F at home. Daughter V took so much time off from work that she lost her job. She had to move into Mrs. F's home with her children as well.

Mrs. F suffered leg ulcers that did not heal despite home nursing and another hospital stay for antibiotics. Doctors had to amputate Mrs. F's leg, so she would not die from the infection. Her memory and stamina were so poor that she could not participate in physical therapy, nor learn to use a prosthetic leg. Again, the doctors recommended 24-hour care in a nursing home.

The daughters knew they were overwhelmed by Mrs. F's care needs and they reluctantly considered nursing home care. Both daughters were under the impression that Medicare would cover all costs, but when the social worker told them the house would have to be sold, or rented at full market value, they quickly changed their minds about nursing home placement. (See Chapter 10: Nursing Home Financing)

****

Financial Exploitation

A conflict of interest arises when caregivers are financially dependent on the people they care for.

****

Daughters V and L discovered that they would have to sell Mrs. F's house to support their mother's nursing home care. Neither daughter had resources to pay rent in Mrs. F's home, or anywhere else, so the daughters took their mother home.

One morning, when the daughters tried to lift Mrs. F out of the bathtub, she lost her balance and everyone fell. Mrs. F broke her hip and arm. One daughter strained her back and the other daughter broke her wrist. Despite Mrs. F's fall, Daughters V and L continued to refuse the recommended nursing home placement. Mrs. F's injury and the daughters' refusal resulted in an investigation by Adult Protective Services (APS).

Since the daughters were not financially independent, their needs and Mrs. F's were in conflict. Mrs. F needed to pay for 24-hour skilled nursing care. If the daughters agreed, they and their children would be homeless. Mrs. F's Social Security check and her small pension would go to the nursing home. The daughters were both unemployed with several children to support; they relied on these funds to help make ends meet.

Mrs. F's daughters did not see their behavior as elder abuse and neglect, but that is what it was. Their failure to provide the care Mrs. F's doctors recommended constitutes neglect. Even though their intentions were good, by relying on Mrs. F's home and pension to support themselves and their children, Daughters V and L committed financial exploitation.(39,40,) This category of elder abuse and neglect arises when seniors' resources are used for anything other than their direct care. (See DO Grow Up; Cover Your Own Expenses)

Luckily, this family lived in a state where the APS program began the investigation of elder abuse and neglect with social services, rather than law enforcement. Social workers helped Daughters V and L find childcare and subsidized housing. This freed both daughters to find employment and Mrs. F's assets were released to support the care she needed.

****

DO NOT Sacrifice Your Income

You should not risk losing your job to give care. You should not quit, or reduce your working hours to the point where your income cannot support your current needs.

DO NOT Bankrupt Your Future.

You should not use a major portion of your funds for eldercare until you have invested the maximum amount in your pension plan and the funds are fully vested. You have to be sure you will have enough money to meet your needs in retirement. (See DO Plan for Your Own Senior Years)

DO NOT Forget Age-Appropriate Insurance.

You should not spend a major portion of your money on eldercare unless you have **health insurance** and other types of insurance appropriate to your age. At the beginning of the adult years, **disability insurance** protects your most important asset; it protects the income that makes all other assets possible. You need to insure your assets with coverage for your home or apartment, your car and other valuables. Everyone should plan for funeral expenses. Yes, young adults, even you. A financial planner can help decide whether you need a small insurance policy, specific burial insurance, or another investment strategy to cover this unexpected need.

As soon as you have dependents who would suffer financially from your death, you will need a larger **life insurance** policy. You may want to pay off a home to ease the financial burden on your surviving spouse. There may be children who need to be educated, or parents who need care if you are not there to care for them. Again, the advice of a financial planner is critical. There are different types of policies and each type has a different impact on your overall financial plan.

Your insurance needs change as you approach retirement and as your dependents age. Once your dependents become independent, or pass away, they will not need your income. Then, you may want to shift some of the life insurance and disability insurance costs into **long-term care insurance** premiums. Long-term care insurance supports care that is not covered by Medicare or other health insurance. This may include the deductibles and co-payments that patients must pay as part of health insurance contracts, home care that does not require skilled nurses, assisted-living and supportive-care facilities, or adult day care services.

Many financial advisors recommend that long-term care insurance should become a priority between age 50 and 55. Below this age, you may pay more in premiums than you might ever use for long-term care. Over age 60, long-term care insurance premiums are usually very expensive.

Be careful about getting all of your information from someone who sells insurance only. Discuss your insurance needs with financial planning professionals who can advise you on your total financial plan (budgeting and debt management, investing, wealth building and retirement planning). The services of these professionals can be expensive, but many churches, libraries, local colleges and community centers offer classes at little or no cost. In some communities, financial professionals offer their services at fees calculated on a sliding scale, based on income.

DO Grow Up; Cover Your Own Expenses.

Your parents' resources are for them. They earned the money; they saved the money and it should be used to take care of them. They do not have to leave the money to you. Conflicts of interest arise when a caregiver has any level of financial dependence on the senior. This can lead to financial exploitation. The conflict is obvious when caregivers divert the senior's pension to cover a drug, or gambling habit. The conflict is blatant when adult children do not support themselves financially. They have no other visible means of support, yet they live in the family home free of charge. They also eat, use the phone, drive the car, watch cable or satellite TV and enjoy other costly resources without contributing to the household finances.

The conflict of interest can also be more subtle. Instead of paying for adult day care as the doctor recommended, perhaps a caregiver uses the senior's money to pay a child's school tuition. It is inappropriate to create a situation where seniors' money is not available to provide the care they need. It does not matter that the caregiver uses money for a legal purpose. When caregivers divert seniors' financial resources for any reason other than the seniors' direct care, (assuming the senior either did not consent, or is not capable of consent), this constitutes elder mistreatment in the category of financial exploitation. In most states, financial exploitation **is** illegal and it carries serious law enforcement consequences.(41)

DO Make Their Home Equity Work for Them.

Your parents' property belongs to them. They paid for it; they maintained it and the equity should be used to provide for their care. Reverse mortgages make the equity in a home available to finance caregiving while the senior still lives in the house. These are not home equity loans to be repaid; at the person's death, the home belongs to the bank, not to the heirs. Most reverse mortgage programs have a provision to allow life-long residence even if the senior outlives the equity in the home. Estate planners, attorneys, realtors and banks have information about reverse mortgages. AGAIN, other people who live in the house must prepare to meet their own housing needs. These people either have to buy the house, or arrange to live elsewhere.

DO Realize They Don't Owe You Anything.

Eldercare advocates recommend that the dedicated caregivers who jeopardize their incomes should receive assistance in the form of tax credits, Medicare and Social Security benefits. Unfortunately, I have encountered people who believe caregiving earns them free access to all of a senior's assets. If you think your seniors **owe** you a living, become a professional. Some eldercare agencies will hire family members, train them and assign them to their own seniors (possibly, along with other clients). If you are giving care from your heart, you don't require payment.

DO Plan for Your Own Senior Years.

Make your children's caregiving responsibilities easier than your parents have made yours. Invest in long-term care insurance, prepare a will and give someone the legal right to make medical and financial decisions on your behalf if you become disabled. Let family members know where your important papers are and tell them what you wish for your last days. (See Chapter 7: Advance Directives)

If your family has generational wealth, money and property intended for transfer to future generations, you should work to shelter those resources in the appropriate type of trust. An estate planner can help you do this early in your adult years.

Emotional Health: The Mind You Save May Be Your Own.

The challenge of eldercare can be emotionally draining. Caregivers may experience disappointment, anger, guilt and fear. These emotions are more powerful because of fatigue. Depression is more common in caregivers than in other people,[42] but there are ways to strengthen your emotional state.

Don't Lean on Reeds: Avoid Disappointment.

In <u>Jesus in Blue Jeans</u>[42], Laurie Beth Jones describes traits in Jesus' personality that can help people of any faith, or spiritual persuasion to live fuller lives. In the chapter "He Did Not Lean on Reeds," Ms. Jones cautions us not to continually rely on people who prove to be unreliable.

****

Mr. E has three daughters who live at opposite corners of a triangle that covers the entire metropolitan area. Daughter R is the middle daughter. She and her own daughters (Mr. E's granddaughters) take turns taking care of Mr. E without any help from Daughter R's sisters. The oldest sister has a hectic work schedule. The youngest sister is very upset about Mr. E's illness and she admits, "I can't handle this."

Whenever caregiving options arise, instead of making the distance convenient for her, Daughter R always looks for resources in the center of the region "to make it easier for all of us to get there." Daughter R gets angry when she must travel a long distance to visit Mr. E while the others "don't even come to see about Dad." Daughter R has close friends who offer to run errands and care for Mr. E, so Daughter R can rest, or take a vacation. Daughter R usually refuses this help saying with disapproval, "Dad has three children. He shouldn't have to get care from strangers." Daughter R plays out this cycle with every new care decision and she burns herself out in the process.

****

Daughter R is leaning on reeds. She could save herself disappointment, anger and stress if she would accept that her sisters are not going to do what she wants them to do. Daughter R should arrange her dad's care in a way that is convenient for her and her daughters, the people who actually provide the care.

Instead of leaning on reeds, Daughter R should stand on rocks, the friends who are her real support system. Daughter R's friends offer to help and she should accept. In refusing the help, Daughter R devalues her friends' offers and she devalues herself. Many of Daughter R's friends never met her father; they are acting out of love for Daughter R.

The definition of "family" goes beyond blood. My grandmother always said, "there's no should, there's only is." It doesn't matter who **should** do it. The important thing is: who **is** doing it. Get help where you can get it, not just where you want it. If people prove unreliable, stop relying on them.

Avoid Guilt.

Guilt can sap your energy. You will be a better caregiver and a healthier one when you refuse to succumb to guilt. Remember Mrs. F and her daughters V and L from earlier in this chapter (See Financial Exploitation). There were numerous opportunities for Daughter V to feel guilty. She could have wrung her hands and cried about how she let everyone down. Instead, she tried to make the best of everything.

****

After Mrs. F went into the nursing home, Daughter V went back to work and she was able to visit her mom only two or three times a week. When she visited, Daughter V read her mom's favorite bible stories, sang her favorite hymns, or played recordings of the musicians Mrs. F liked. It broke Daughter V's heart that she could not be at the nursing home everyday, but she traded off with her sister, Daughter L, and a couple of trusted friends; someone was with Mrs. F every day.

Daughter V made sure she had breakfast, or dinner with her kids each day. On Fridays, she and the kids made tacos or pizza. They popped popcorn and watched a video together. They also had a special dinner every Sunday. Daughter V made an event of every moment she spent with her kids. She had breakfast with her girlfriends on Saturday mornings while the kids did chores and she went out with other friends two Saturday evenings each month.

****

Several strategies will help you avoid guilt and its negative impact on your emotional health.

Keep your "I LOVE YOUs" up to date.

Show you care for everyone who needs you by giving your best in little ways. Daughter V kept her "I LOVE YOUs" up to date by finding ways to make special time for her kids, her mom and herself. When you keep your "I LOVE YOUs" up to date, you will not have regrets to add to your grief when your loved one is gone.

It's OK to change lanes when you get a clue.

Sometimes, you get new information that forces you to change course. Even though they had said "never" to nursing home placement, after their mom fell, Daughters V and L had to admit their situation wasn't really working for anybody. Don't feel guilty when you have to change the plan.

You can only do what you can do.

Give yourself credit for doing what you can. Even though Daughter V wasn't giving everybody everything she wanted to give, she knew she was doing her best.

Guilt is the most worthless emotion. Guilt hurts you and it does not help your loved ones at all. Take steps to avoid another worthless and unproductive sentiment.

Say "No" to Self-Pity. Don't whine; hum.

Laurie Beth Jones also says, "He Didn't Whine; He Hummed."[43] Some caregivers whine, "See how hard I'm working? See how much I've sacrificed?" These caregivers need to accept this simple fact:

It's hard to get kicked in the backside, if you don't bend over.

You accepted the caregiving role. Many caregivers say "I have no choice; nobody else will do it," but there is a choice.

What about the family members who don't help? They have chosen **not** to give care, haven't they? When you admit you have chosen to be a caregiver, you have power to stop whining. Then, you can hum like a well-oiled machine; you can develop your support system (See Chapters: 2 through 4) and you can move on to successful, healthy caregiving.

****

Daughter K has been the primary caregiver for her dad for 3 years. Dad openly preferred Daughter K's brothers as the children grew up. Dad ignored Daughter K; he never supported her and he took no notice when she moved out of the house. She felt abandoned. When Dad became ill, the boys planned on nursing home placement, but Daughter K refused to allow it. She moved back home to care for Dad. She called her brothers frequently, crying that she had given up her dreams and her life to care for Dad, even though he didn't love her. She took every opportunity to make sure Dad knew it, too.

Daughter K's neighbors called Adult Protective Services (APS) when they heard yelling, followed by a loud crash. The investigators found that Dad had pushed Daughter K into a bookcase and she had shoved back. The elder abuse program in this state used a social service model instead of immediately involving law enforcement. APS social workers offered adult day care for Dad and counseling for the caregiver. Through counseling, Daughter K realized that her motivation for moving back home had been to show Dad she was a good child. She needed to prove that she deserved his love, not his neglect, or contempt. Eventually, she accepted that she could never earn her father's approval. She also learned that whining to her brothers would not get them to sympathize, or to help.

Daughter K made an active decision to continue as Dad's caregiver and having chosen this road, she felt more empowered. She accepted adult day care for her Dad and she went back to school. She was more patient and less needy in her interactions with Dad and he became less agitated. Daughter K cared for Dad every night and she took advantage of respite care services when she needed to be away.

****

Most of you are not legal guardians. Even if you are a spouse, even if there are no other family members, you are not **legally** obligated to give care (although, once you step into the caregiving role, many states will recognize you as the legal caregiver for investigations of elder abuse and neglect). You have **chosen** not to mistreat, or abandon your senior. You have **chosen** to be the caregiver. Get over it! Embrace your choice to give care. Stop whining and hummm-motoring on, getting the help you need, taking care of yourself and doing the job well.

Tell the Truth, At Least To Yourself.

It's OK to dislike caregiving. It's even OK to dislike your seniors. It's OK to resent caregiving and admit you are overwhelmed.

It is dangerous to deny or ignore your feelings, so find a useful, safe place to tell the truth. This is not whining or humming; it's preventive maintenance. It may not be a good idea to confide in family members and it is almost never a good idea to confide in the dependent senior. Behavioral health professionals can help you deal with the feelings more quickly. Counselors can also help you move the feelings into an area where they do less emotional damage. Caregiver support groups, social workers, geriatric care managers, clergy and mental health counselors are important resources.

Get Help to Save Your Mind.

Don't be afraid of mental health professionals. I don't think you're crazy. You may be functioning well, but stress makes caregiving cost too much, emotionally. When your car isn't running well, do you always fix it yourself? Do you rebuild the engine, knock out all of the dents and touch up the paint? All of us hire people to do something in our lives. Given unlimited time and the right manuals, we could probably do everything we hire other people to do, but why would we? Professionals have been trained to fill those roles. When we accept their help, we free up our time and energy for other things.

Try to look at behavioral health counselors in the same way. Given unlimited time, you could work through your guilt, sadness, anger and other emotions, but working through the feelings on your own isn't a good use of your time.

You **will** have to work through the feelings. When you try to ignore and bury feelings, you compress them. The feelings become more powerful; they overwhelm you and they always come out eventually.(44) The feelings don't always explode; sometimes, they ooze out through your voice when you snap at co-workers, or people you love. Negative feelings can erode your sleep and cause you to overeat. You cannot ignore the negative feelings.

Medications for the Mind

Depression and anxiety are common responses to caregiver stress. Many medications are available to treat depression and anxiety. These medicines can be very useful when they are prescribed by a skilled primary care physician, or a psychiatrist and they are used along with counseling. Many of my patients worry about becoming "addicted" to these medicines, but are people with diabetes addicted to the medications that control their blood sugar? Are people who have high blood pressure addicted to their blood pressure medicine? No, people with diabetes and hypertension need a chemical adjustment. When depression and anxiety interfere with life function, many people need a chemical adjustment. Antidepressant and anti-anxiety medications can help achieve this adjustment.

Some people need medication for only a short time, while others may need it for the rest of their lives. Depression is a physical ailment, not a character flaw. A trained professional will be able to monitor the medications, maximize the benefits and minimize any risks.

Spiritual Health: Put on the Armor of Inner Peace; Wield the Sword of Forgiveness.

Caregiver survival depends on a strong inner spirit that protects itself from despair; the spirit finds joyful purpose, sees the big picture, avoids guilt and knows when to let go. This kind of spirit is also strong enough to forgive.

Find Joy Outside of Caregiving

You are more than a caregiver; you will be a better caregiver if you nurture the other parts of your life.

****

Daughter A cares for her mother, Mrs. W. Daughter A makes use of adult day care and she gets help from respite volunteers in her church. This support allows Daughter A to participate in a bowling league and sing in the church choir.

****

Grandson N cares for his grandmother. He found an adult day care center with early evening and weekend hours so he can study Taekwondo after work two nights each week. On Saturday, he teaches this martial art to kids at the youth center. Grandson N has also pulled together a business team to help him open his own Taekwondo school.

****

Mr. McR sings in a barbershop quartet. His group performs in his community and at his wife's nursing home. He takes Mrs. McR out to lunch, to concerts and to seminars at the local library. He also mentors troubled teenagers.

****

Daughter-in-law Q cares for her mother-in-law, Mrs. B. Daughter-in-law Q hires a respite worker two mornings per week. She alternates taking a yoga class, getting a massage, having coffee with friends and participating in a book club. Once a year, she makes use of the respite program in an assisted-living facility and she spends a week enjoying the fall leaves in Michigan.

****

Find Purpose Outside of Caregiving.

Do you have talents and interests outside of caregiving that could bring you joy, or help someone else? Lift your head up; look out from your misery and be a blessing to someone outside of your situation.

If you cannot think of a place to pitch in, please consider working with teens and pre-teens. Today's young people face challenges most of us have never faced, even as adults. They deal with much more violence and peer pressure than we did as kids. Parents are working themselves to death; grandparents and other family members may be in another part of the country. Divorce, job transfers and the increased mobility of our society have eroded the stability of neighborhoods and relationships.

The kids have few resources. Most after-school programs accommodate kids only up to age 12. Many kids from age 13 to 18 are without adult supervision for 3 or 4 hours, until their parents come home from work. These kids are vulnerable to violence and the consequences of experimenting with alcohol, drugs and sex.

We cannot overestimate the wisdom and support kids can get from sane, responsible adults. Share your wisdom through a homework hotline, a foster grandparent program, a church, a community center, or a school. Pitch in and push your community leaders to start an after-school program that meets the need!

"Threads in a Tapestry:" See the Big Picture.

Regardless of your spiritual orientation, caregiving is easier when you can believe your specific trial is part of something bigger. "Threads in a Tapestry" is a popular song that was written years ago. The song still reminds us that we are each threads in the tapestry of life with our own special and essential function. We see only our little corner of the tapestry and sometimes, our corner looks pretty bad, but we can take comfort in believing that **Someone** sees the whole tapestry. We don't have to understand it all; we just have to be the best thread we can be in our little corner. **Someone** understands everything and makes sure the entire tapestry makes beautiful sense.

Your Test Becomes Your Testimony; Your Mess Becomes Your Ministry.

Many spiritual leaders use this phrase to help people understand that good can come from life challenges; everything happens for a reason. Your testimony is not that you survive walking through trouble. Your testimony is **how** you walk through the trouble. Get your head up above your own misery and be a blessing to somebody else.

I am not asking you to take on more direct caregiving responsibility. I want you to look for joy in your current situation and share it. Despite the trouble, can you look for the lesson in your situation? Despite your grief, can you find something positive there for yourself, for your senior, for someone else? That is your testimony. What have you learned in your struggle? Can you use that knowledge to help another caregiver who is toiling farther back on the road you have already traveled? That is your ministry.

You protect yourself from despair when you can feel joy in the face of hardship. Show joy and you can inspire other caregivers to hold on.

God Always Answers Prayer; Sometimes the Answer is NO.

Even when you do everything you can, sometimes things don't work the way you want them to.

****

Mr. and Mrs. O'C were in their 80s. They lived alone in a large, beautiful home that they cared for with great pride. Neither Mr. nor Mrs. O'C had any memory problems. They were both retired postal workers, living on a good pension. Mrs. O'C paid the bills and Mr. O'C managed their portfolio of investments. The O'Cs had two adult children who lived out of town, but their primary support was Niece Z who lived in the area. Niece Z helped the O'Cs with grocery shopping; she drove them to church and she took them out for dinner every Sunday. Teenagers from the church put the trash out, cut the grass and shoveled the snow.

For the past few years Mr. and Mrs. O'C suffered declining health. Mr. O'C developed severe arthritis in his hips, knees and back. Pain made it difficult for him to walk and he had trouble taking care of his personal needs. Mrs. O'C suffered several heart attacks that left her very weak. Shortness of breath and leg swelling kept her in a recliner most of the day and night.

The seniors looked to Niece Z for more help. When they could no longer negotiate the basement stairs, they called on

Niece Z to do their laundry. Neither senior could get to the bathroom in time, so the laundry was quite a chore. Within a year, Niece Z also shouldered responsibility for housekeeping and taking care of the dogs. She cooked several times each week and she provided transportation to doctor appointments for both seniors.

Niece Z knew her aunt and uncle had a good income. They also had significant equity in their home. Even so, Mrs. O'C refused when her niece suggested they hire a housekeeper/companion. "We won't let strangers into our house. You are our family. We don't trust anybody else." They also balked at the expense. Niece Z suggested they apply for a reverse mortgage to get the funds to hire the help they needed, but Mr. O'C said, "the bank will never take my house out from under me." According to Mrs. O'C, that was that.

Niece Z was in her early 60's and she had medical problems of her own. She struggled with diabetes and painful arthritis that affected her back and knees. At Christmastime, Niece Z's children came into town and they were amazed to see their mother looking so frail. They asked her to come to live with them so they could see to her golden years. Niece Z could not consider leaving town without settling things for her aunt and uncle; she refused to go with her children, but she did agree to look into getting more help for the O'Cs.

Niece Z arranged for the seniors to see a local geriatrician who confirmed that each senior was of sound mind. The geriatrician recommended a geriatric care manager to help with hiring in-home help and other services, but the O'Cs refused to spend the money. Niece Z called the local area agency on aging. The housekeeping service charged a fee based on income, but the O'Cs' income was too high for them to get the services free of charge. Even though this service was less expensive than the private care manager, Mr. and Mrs. O'C still refused. Niece Z called the O'Cs' children, but they said, "Mom and Dad are always alright." The children had busy lives of their own.

Over the next six months, Niece Z took so much pain medicine that her stomach began to hurt. Physical therapy had not been successful and injections for pain management provided only temporary relief. Her doctor recommended back surgery, but Niece Z knew the recuperation time was at least six weeks; she was sure disaster would strike if she were unavailable to the O'Cs for that long. She put off the surgery.

One day, when she was walking down into the basement to do the laundry, Niece Z's left leg became weak and she fell down the stairs. She was lucky. There were no broken bones, but her doctor found that arthritis in her back had pinched the nerves that controlled her leg. This was the last straw.

Niece Z made arrangements to sell her home and move to the town where her children lived. She planned to have her surgery there and stay with them while she recuperated. Then, she would find a condo of her own nearby. She called the O'Cs' children and told them she planned to leave in one month. She gave them a package that contained the names, addresses and telephone numbers of the geriatrician, the geriatric care manager and the other resources she had collected.

When Niece Z told her aunt and uncle about her plans, both seniors were furious. "After all we've done for you, you can just walk out on us like this?" Mr. and Mrs. O'C had raised their niece and she thought of them as her parents. Niece Z was sorry her aunt and uncle were disappointed in her and it hurt that they thought she was ungrateful. Still, she had her own health to consider and she told them so.

Niece Z reminded the O'Cs that they had worked hard and saved their money. They were more than capable of making arrangements to take care of themselves. She called the department on aging and she arranged to be present when the social worker came to visit. Unfortunately, the O'Cs refused to talk to the social worker. Niece Z continued to bring food, but she stopped doing the laundry and the housekeeping.

At the end of the month, Niece Z said goodbye and she left town. She called once a week to say hello and to answer any questions about whom the O'Cs should call for help. She also talked to their children who had started to get calls from their parents and from the neighbors. The children took leave from their jobs, and flew into town to see about their parents. No matter what the O'Cs or their children said, Niece Z did not feel guilty and she did not take their panic to heart. She gave information and empathy. She underwent successful back surgery and she enjoyed the love and support of her family.

****

You did everything you were supposed to do. You admitted there was a problem; you approached the challenge directly and you acted right on time. You saw the geriatrician to get a level of care prescription. You asked your family for help with specific requests. You listened to your seniors' requests with adult ears. (See Chapter 6: When the Doctor Says It's Not Safe for Your Loved One To…: Balance Independence and Safety).You made the best use of your resources and you did what you needed to do, but he **still** won't take the medicine; she **still** won't eat properly; they **still** won't cooperate with care and family members **still** won't show up when they say they will.

A geriatric assessment will let you know if seniors have mental problems. If they are not mentally capable, call either the local Adult Protective Services program, or the Office of the Public Guardian (an attorney who works for the state and supervises guardianship petitions). If the seniors have no mental problems, they are allowed to make bad decisions. Some states have laws on self-neglect, but usually if a senior knows what he is doing and he refuses help, little can be done. There comes a point when you have to accept that, at least right now, the answer is **NO**. Things may have to get worse before they can get better.

You did your best, let God do the rest.

Give notice and step aside. Sometimes, other caregivers will step up. Sometimes, the only thing you can do is keep your eyes and ears open. When the person is ready to accept the help she needs, you can step back in. Either way, conserve your energy and take care of yourself.

The Angry Caregiver

> "Fear leads to anger; anger leads to hate;
> hate leads to suffering."

Yoda, in "Star Wars, Episode I: The Phantom Menace"

What if they weren't good parents?

Caregiving can be especially painful when the people you care for did not take good care of you. (45)

****

Miss X brought her mother, Mrs. McL, to the geriatric assessment center for evaluation of memory loss. Mrs. McL was 78 years old. She was a robust and stern woman who had been confined to a wheelchair for more than ten years, because diabetes damaged the nerves in her legs. Miss X was an only child and she had also supervised the care of her father until he died from Parkinson's disease two years earlier.

The geriatrics team noted that Miss X was very quiet and she seemed nervous. She was in constant motion, anticipating her mother's need for tissues, water and snacks. She frequently changed Mrs. McL's position in the wheelchair to be sure that her mother was comfortable. Miss X said very little in Mrs. McL's presence, but when she was interviewed alone, Miss X demonstrated that she was a knowledgeable and capable caregiver. She admitted that she was stressed, but she expressed no hope that things could change.

At the end of the first evaluation, the geriatric nurse practitioner accompanied both women to the parking lot to help Mrs. McL into the car. The nurse asked a question and both women answered simultaneously. Mrs. McL screamed, "don't interrupt," and she backhanded Miss X, sending her sprawling onto the pavement.

Miss X was even quieter in the follow-up visit and the geriatrics team thought she looked more tired and stressed than she had before. Mrs. McL refused adult day care, respite services and in-home help. This time, Miss X refused a separate interview. Her mother laughed when the social worker recommended counseling, but Miss X said nothing. The team arranged for a social worker from the community department on aging to visit the home. Everyone worried that it was only a matter of time before something terrible happened.

Several months later, Miss X went to bed without cleaning the kitchen. She had felt very tired for several weeks. She was unable to eat very much, because her stomach was always queasy even though she chewed antacid tablets all day.

The next morning, Mrs. McL screamed at Miss X about the dirty dishes, but instead of rushing to wash them as she would have done in the past, Miss X sat at the kitchen table. She just did not have the energy to move. Mrs. McL rolled up to Miss X and raised her hand. This time, Miss X twisted her mother's wrist hard enough to leave a bruise. As Mrs. McL yelped in pain, Miss X doubled over and collapsed to the floor.

Miss X was hospitalized with a bleeding ulcer that required a blood transfusion. No one was available to take care of Mrs. McL so the local area agency on aging arranged for her to move into an assisted-living facility for the disabled. Mrs. McL agreed, because "it's just until the girl gets better." However, Mrs. McL stayed in assisted-living, because Miss X decided to travel around the country with a missionary program from her church.

****

In <u>Drama of the Gifted Child</u>, (46) Dr. Alice Miller tells us about "unconditional love" tanks that must be filled by a specific time in a child's development. When parents are inadequate or abusive, this special time passes and these particular tanks can never be filled. Adult love tanks can be filled, but many people try to fill the childhood tanks as adults. This behavior can bring disastrous consequences to their relationships, careers and overall happiness.

According to Miller, the effects of unhealthy parenting can either stop, or they can continue to the next generation. I believe the impact can also go backwards, causing elder abuse or neglect. If a previously abused child/caregiver identifies with the parent in an abusive relationship, the caregiver is more likely to strike out; she remembers being defenseless and unable to strike out as a child. This caregiver may feel, "now I'm in control; I won't let him hurt me ever again." If the caregiver identifies with the abused child, she also recalls the hurt, but she says "I'm in control; I'll make sure she never feels the way I felt." The second caregiver is able to stop what Miller calls "the cycle of contempt."

If parents knew better, they'd do better.

I do not believe most parents intend to hurt their children; kids don't come with an operator's manual. Unlike driving and other adult responsibilities, parenting does not require pre-screening, training, or a license. It is also difficult for parents to do a good job when they had poor role models in parenting.

By now, you've had YOU longer than your parents had YOU.

Many caregivers explain their unhappiness, or excuse their behavior because their parents treated them badly, but most people are well past legal age by the time they become caregivers. They are adults and they have had the opportunity to work through memories that cause emotional turmoil. Adults are responsible for seeking professional help in overcoming the impact of unhealthful parenting. If your life is not all you want it to be, is this still your parents' fault?

The Angry Spouse

Sometimes, a caregiver is responsible to care for a spouse with whom she shared a long, unhappy marriage.

****

Mr. and Mrs. Q married 50 years ago when he was a 30 year-old attorney and she was an 18 year-old high school graduate. Mr. Q had a brilliant career and Mrs. Q was the perfect homemaker, mother and hostess, but as their four children grew up, Mrs. Q yearned for a different life. Mr. Q ridiculed his wife's intelligence throughout their marriage. He also belittled her efforts to return to school, to develop her interests, or find employment. Despite this, Mrs. Q turned her love of crafting into a successful shop where she gave lessons and sold crafting supplies. She became active in the chamber of commerce and eventually, she was inducted into the local business hall of fame. Mr. Q was never supportive and once he retired from the law, he was very vocal in resenting Mrs. Q's interests outside of their home.

Mr. Q suffered a stroke that left him confused and unsteady on his feet. Mrs. Q took excellent care of Mr. Q. She never left him alone; she took him to her shop, to meetings and on outings with friends. The Q's children arranged for a geriatric assessment when Mr. Q became sexually inappropriate with Mrs. Q in public.

The geriatrics team noticed that Mr. Q was loud and friendly; he chuckled as he talked about "keeping the little woman in line." Mrs. Q was very quiet, but she smiled sweetly as she allowed her children to do the talking.

The geriatrician found that Mr. Q had a strange bruise. Mrs. Q explained that her husband had fallen, but the team thought this was unlikely. How could Mr. Q fall in such a way that a long, linear bruise slashed across his chest?

Mrs. Q broke down in tears. She admitted that Mr. Q had been physically and psychologically abusive throughout their marriage; he had assaulted her frequently with sexual demands. Mrs. Q had made plans to divorce Mr. Q, but when he suffered the stroke, she did not feel she could leave him.

Mrs. Q was committed to giving care, but she had little time for herself; she was overwhelmed by her husband's demands and by memories of a lifetime of abuse. This time, when he accosted her, Mrs. Q hit him with his cane. She struck out as she had never done in the previous 50 years.

The children agreed to support any course of action their mother chose, but she decided to continue caregiving. The team arranged counseling for Mrs. Q to help her release years of repressed anger. They also arranged adult day care and respite care for Mr. Q, so Mrs. Q could have time to enjoy her life.

****

The Cycle of Abuse

A caregiver's response to abuse can damage everyone whether the caregiver was abused as a child, or as an adult.

Caregivers can:

- Fear past, or current abuse from the senior (like Miss X)

- They can wear themselves out to prove they are worthy of love and undeserving of contempt. (See Daughter K in Chapter 4: Don't Whine. Hum.)

- They might work too hard, worrying that they could give too little care in subconscious revenge. (possible motivation for Miss X, Daughter K and Mrs. Q)

- They could become abusive themselves, whether anger and revenge are conscious or not (possible for all of the above caregivers).

That ship has already sailed.

Caregivers may not be able to make peace with seniors who hurt them. Mental or physical illness may move the senior beyond the reach of conversations that could bring resolution. Unresolved feelings of anger and revenge can make caregivers mistreat seniors, children, employees, students and other people who may not be able to defend themselves.

The people you care for may have hurt you when you were defenseless, but hurting them cannot heal your emotional wounds; it only perpetuates evil. Is that justice?

If you are an angry caregiver, get professional help to find closure within yourself. Grieve empty childhood love tanks and accept that they will not be filled. Fill adult love tanks today, through healthy relationships and activities that do not involve your seniors.

You must make other arrangements for seniors' care if you cannot find a way to deal with your anger. Get out of the caregiving situation for your senior's sake and for your own sake.

The Power of Forgiveness

<u>When Forgiveness Doesn't Make Sense</u>,(47) is a powerful book by Robert M. Jeffress. The author says forgiveness is essential for emotional and spiritual health, but it has nothing to do with the person who injures you.

****

Remember Daughter R and her sisters (Chapter 4: Don't Lean on Reeds). In addition to being inconvenienced and overwhelmed, Daughter R spent a lot of time complaining to her husband, her kids and her friends about her sisters. "I can't believe they ignore Dad this way. He worked hard to give us a good childhood and he was always there for them. It's just so unfair. My oldest sister has a lot of money. There's no reason why she can't hire a nurse one afternoon a week to give me a break. The baby sister, well she doesn't do anything at all. You can't tell me she can't come down to see Dad." Daughter R cried and she worked herself up into regular frenzies, because she was so angry with her sisters. Her anger made her unhappy, but her frenzies had absolutely no effect on her sisters, or their behavior.

****

Jeffress tells us forgiveness does not excuse any behavior; forgiveness does not mean it is OK for people to hurt, or disappoint us. Neither does forgiveness mean you have to stay in the line of fire. You do not have to let the situation continue. You can remove yourself, or at least remove your feelings. Forgiveness does not require the offenders to be sorry, or even to recognize the need to be forgiven. Forgiveness just takes the knife out of your heart so the situation has no further power to hurt you.

The first step in forgiveness is to stop judging your family members. You don't really know why they won't help. Maybe they can't. Maybe the person who was such a good mother to you wasn't such a good mother to your sister. It's possible that the loved one was such a wonderful grandfather that your brother can't bear to see him weakening. You can never know the true status of a relationship that doesn't involve you. Even if you think you know, your opinion isn't relevant. What actually happened in the relationship doesn't matter. What matters is what the involved parties **believe** happened. When it comes to motivating behavior, feelings might as well be facts. You can't dispute the feelings.

You can't decide what other people owe your senior. You can't spend other people's time and you can't spend their money. There is no way for you to fully understand the other responsibilities that people have and you can't order their priorities. How would you respond if other family members told you what to do with, or for your senior? What if they told you to spend **less** time giving care? How would you respond? Would their opinions change your behavior?

Jeffress says "unforgiveness" can destroy you. Let bitterness go and forgive family members who don't help. You can't judge their feelings and you can't control their behavior, but through forgiveness, you can change your reaction and stop letting the situation hurt you.

You can deal with negative emotions between you and other family members through counseling after your loved one is gone. Don't try to do it now. Don't waste the time, or the energy you need to take care of your senior and yourself.

The tapestry of life is larger than your own thread, but each thread is important. Be the strongest thread you can be by protecting your physical, financial, emotional and spiritual health. Then, you can contribute to the beauty of the whole tapestry, the "big picture."

CHAPTER 5: WHEN ELDERCARE PUTS OTHER RELATIONSHIPS AT RISK

Caregiving can consume so much of your energy that you have no time for other relationships. Deciding how to juggle these commitments can be stressful for everyone involved.

****

What is at Risk? Your Marriage and Family

When Mr. T's mother became bedridden after a stroke, he decided against admitting her to a nursing home. He insisted that his wife quit her job to care for his mom, but his wife was soon exhausted. Mr. T did not want strangers to care for his mom and he refused respite services. In the next year, Mr. T's wife developed lupus (an illness that left her tired and in pain). She was no longer able to handle things alone. Mr. T insisted their two teenagers give up their activities to help out after school and on weekends. The kids became increasingly sullen and their school performance suffered.

Fatigue and resentment undermined the communication and intimacy in the T's marriage. When Mr. T's wife announced her intent to file for divorce and move to her sister's home with the children, Mr. T realized he didn't want to lose his family.

Mr. T called the local department on aging and he found that his mother was eligible for caregiver service 4 hours every weekday. He paid for an adult day care center for the other weekday hours and he asked church members to help every other weekend. He was also able to afford a week of respite care twice a year. Mr. T's wife and kids still pitched in, but their responsibilities rotated with the hired caregiver's duties. They all had time for themselves and for each other.

****

Your Children

When Mother first came to live with us, my daughter was about 18 months old. One weekend, my daughter was hospitalized for a stomach virus that caused massive diarrhea and dehydration. My husband and I made a commitment that our daughter would never wake up in the hospital without seeing a familiar face. Our friends helped us take shifts to make this possible.

One Sunday, my husband had to work and none of our friends were available to be at the hospital with my daughter, or to stay with my mother. We knew it was not safe to leave Mother alone at home. She placed a dishtowel on the stovetop and when it caught fire, she just stood there, looking at it. The smoke detector screeched. Our five-year old son ran to get the fire extinguisher and he yelled to my husband and me. Through all this noise, Mother looked at the flames calmly and she said, "Why is this happening? This never happened before." If Mother had been at home alone, she could have died; I had to take her with me.

While the baby was sleeping, Mother insisted on going outside to smoke. At this point in her dementia, Mother thought she knew everybody and she generously offered money to everyone she saw. She could no longer communicate well enough to get assistance if she got lost. The hospital was in a major urban area with all of the attendant dangers; I knew Mother could possibly be mugged, or worse. I did not want to leave the baby, but I could not let Mother go out alone. What an agonizing decision!

There were several nurses on the floor and the baby was in a crib with sides so high that it formed a cage; she would not be able to fall out, or climb out. If my daughter woke while I was gone, she might be frightened, but she would be safe. If I left Mother alone, she would be in danger.

I decided to go with Mother and the next week, I arranged for her to move back to the city where most of our family lives; there were more available caregivers and we could hire people from Mother's church to be with her all the time. I did not want to be in the position of having to choose between my mother and my children ever again.

****

Ms. J brought her mother, Mrs. I, to live with her when Mrs. I could no longer live alone. Ms. J's son had a learning disorder with behavior challenges. Mrs. I was very agitated by the boy's energy and she followed him around the house, yelling at him. The boy's teachers reported that he was much more distracted and his behavior was more disruptive since his grandmother joined the household. The boy was punished by losing TV privileges and playtime with his friends, but his grades and behavior continued to decline. One day, Ms. J found her son hiding in the basement crying. He sobbed, "Mommy, I asked her to leave me alone; she just won't leave me alone."

Ms. J moved Mrs. I into an assisted-living facility and she visits her mother several times each week. Sometimes she brings her son and sometimes she visits alone. She also brings Mrs. I home for a weekend every month.

****

The Healthy Parent

Dr. S had been a prominent surgeon and politician in his community. He developed a debilitating illness and he became increasingly frail, but his children refused to let anyone know he was ill.

Mrs. S started to lose her battle with caregiving responsibility. She was short of breath and she was increasingly tired and tearful. The family did not want to risk eroding Dr. S's political power, tarnishing his reputation, or "ruining his legacy," so they refused all caregiving help. One day, Mrs. S noted a strange ache in her shoulders and jaw.

She shrugged it off, took two aspirin and prepared lunch for Dr. S and a visiting colleague. Suddenly, Mrs. S couldn't catch her breath. She was lucky that Dr. S's friend was able to call 911. Mrs. S suffered a mild heart attack. When the family realized how close they came to losing Mom too, they hired help.

****

Your Life

Daughter B had cared for her mother, Mrs. U, for most of her adult life. In her early adulthood, Daughter B fell in love and she became engaged, but she put off her marriage; she put off buying a home and she postponed other life passages. She refused to take vacations with her fiancé, because Mrs. U became ill whenever Daughter B's attention was not fully focused on her.

Daughter B worried that life was passing her by and she became increasingly stressed and depressed. Eventually, she was unable to leave her home. Through supportive psychotherapy, Daughter B was able to see that her mom was being unreasonable. Daughter B learned that she deserved an independent life.

Mrs. U went to adult day care where the caregivers doted on her. Daughter B got married and Mrs. U came to love her son- in-law, because he doted on her also. The couple moved with Mrs. U into a home that had an attached private suite. They used a baby monitor to check on Mrs. U at night. Whenever the couple took a vacation, they hired one of the caregivers from the adult day care privately. Mrs. U grumbled, but she was okay.

****

Pastor Jimmy Evans authored a marriage maintenance resource called <u>Marriage on the Rock: God's Design for</u>

Your Dream Marriage. In this book, Evans teaches that, in families, our first allegiance is to our spouse.(48)

You owe your parents your existence, not your life.

Parents deserve to be treated with love and respect. They should expect reasonable comfort and consideration, but they are not entitled to all of your time, all of your energy, or all of your resources. Never are they entitled at the expense of your marriage and home.

Your Parents vs Your Children

The challenge is especially painful when caregivers have to choose between the generation that created them and the generation they are charged to create. You may be grateful; you might not be who you are today if your parents had not provided for you. Even so, your job is to prepare your children just as your parents prepared you. In the section, "On Children," in The Prophet, Kahlil Gibran helps us put these allegiances into perspective. To paraphrase, Gibran says time circles forward, not backward; the parent's role is to serve as the bow, bent in the Creator's hands so the arrows (children) can fly straight.(49)

Your disabled senior's future is fixed, but your child's future is not. The environment children grow in and the stresses they grow under have a significant impact on their futures. These stressors influence a child's ability to be a citizen, an employee, a spouse, or a parent who can influence future generations. If you have to make a choice, you have to invest in the children.

The Sick Parent vs the Healthy Parent

It can be very painful to try to balance the needs of sick elders and healthy ones, whether the couples are parents, aunts and uncles, siblings or other groups of seniors. Do not penalize the healthy senior for being the last one standing.

See that your healthy loved one gets to do the things he loves, whether he wants to go to a religious service, or a poker game, attend a book club meeting, or travel with friends. There is no way to know how much good time the healthy senior has left. Help healthy elders make the most of their remaining time by helping them to be as happy as they can be.

Of course when there is a health crisis, or if the disabled senior's time is very short, attention will focus on her needs. Everyone will need to adjust for a time. However, when other important relationships continually suffer because you care for a loved one, I believe you have to err on the side of the person who has a healthy future. No matter what you sacrifice, you cannot change the dependent senior's disability and in the case of deteriorating illness, you cannot really change her future.

Don't sacrifice the people who have good time left.

CHAPTER 6: WHEN THE DOCTOR SAYS IT'S NOT SAFE FOR YOUR LOVED ONE TO...: Balance Independence and Safety

Sometimes, the medical facts require a plan of care, but the senior disagrees. It is difficult to give directions to someone who changed your diapers, because this seems to be at odds with the respect and honor our elders are due. Pastor Jimmy Evans writes about relations with elders in <u>Marriage on the Rock</u>. Pastor Evans clarifies the Bible's teaching, "Honor thy father and thy mother,"(50) by pointing out that only children are told to obey(51). You have to hear your seniors' requests with "big-girl" (adult) ears.

One caregiver told me he was uncomfortable insisting on safety with his grandfather. This caregiver had never told an elder what to do; he had been raised to always obey without question. I asked him and I ask you, what would make you more comfortable? **Would you rather have an angry grandfather, or a grandfather who hurts himself, or someone else?**

Dad Shouldn't Drive Anymore.

One of the most difficult problems caregivers face is the need to intervene when a senior can no longer drive safely. Driving is often the last stand of independence and most people strongly resist any effort to limit this activity.

****

Over the past year, Mr. O had several minor accidents on his way to church and to his weekly breakfast with his buddies at the Veterans Hall. He misjudged the distance and hit a car as he changed lanes. He often drove too slowly for the posted speed and he had difficulty staying in his lane.

Even though Mr. O insisted these accidents "could have happened to anybody," his doctor ordered a driving assessment that confirmed several problems. Mr. O's neck mobility was limited by severe arthritis. Extra mirrors failed to solve the problem, because he also suffered from macular degeneration that affected his vision. Mr. O's depth perception, his ability to judge distance and his reflexes were too impaired for him to drive safely.

Mr. O's family consulted a social service agency to help the family find other means of transportation. The agency recommended a combination of family and community resources so Mr. O would not be house bound. The doctor and the family assured Mr. O that he had put in enough time driving everybody else around; now it was his turn to be chauffeured.

When Mr. O still would not agree, the doctor prepared the paperwork to revoke Mr. O's driver's license. Mr. O still drove his car. His wife took the keys. Mr. O had several other sets. Finally, Mr. O's wife and children met with him to tell Mr. O they planned to disable the car for his safety. The family contacted Mr. O's friends and the local mechanic, so no one would assist him in getting the car repaired. Mr. O was angry and he felt betrayed, but he was safe and so were other motorists.

Mr. O refused to go out. Finally, his army buddies descended on his house to read him the riot act about feeling sorry for himself. Did he think he was better than his friends? Hadn't Mr. O driven when Bob had knee surgery? Hadn't he pitched in when Mike broke his foot? Why couldn't they do the same for him? Eventually, Mr. O gave in and his buddies took turns picking him up for their outings.

****

Some families admit that they worry about driving safety, but either they are afraid to intervene, or they do not know how to intervene. This is completely understandable.

Independent driving has been an integral part of our culture since President Eisenhower developed the interstate highway system in the 1950s. Driving is seen as an inalienable right and losing this right can be a life-changing blow to many seniors. Many women in the current generation of older adults have never driven; so, if her spouse can't drive, the woman is also housebound. No wonder families are reluctant to take the car keys!

Many families believe, "It's OK for Dad to drive because Mom is always with him." Mom can't make Dad a safe driver unless she can stop the car. Failure to remove an unsafe driver from the road leads to death. Although seniors drive fewer miles than do people in other age groups, they have more fatal accidents per mile than any age group other than teenagers.[52] Teenagers' driving skills are expected to improve with time and experience. Problems with vision, brain function and mobility cause most of the senior driving difficulties and these conditions get progressively worse over time.

The Special Challenge of Drivers Who Have Memory Loss

Over the past few years, there have been several news reports about horrible accidents involving older drivers. One elderly gentleman drove down a bike path and killed a jogger. Another senior turned onto a highway off-ramp, killing himself and another motorist. An older woman plowed into a group of people standing at a bus stop.

Remember Mr. R in Chapter 2 who got lost on his way to church. He had to detour around a broken water pipe and he could not find the way back to his route. He drove for several hours until he ran out of gas and he was found by the police wandering on a highway 200 miles away from home. Mr. R was terrified and his family spent several hours expecting the worst.

A driving incident is not usually the first sign of memory loss in a senior. Many families admit that, in retrospect worrisome changes occurred long before driving safety became an issue. Did Dad dress differently? Did Mom stop baking, or mismanage her finances? (See Chapter 2 Warning Signs)

Even when memory does not seem "that bad," driving ability can be seriously affected by problems with **executive function**, high level brain activity that involves more than just memory. Executive function involves a complex series of mental steps. The brain takes in new information and filters it through memories stored from past experience. Then, the brain decides how to respond and it selects the resources it needs to respond correctly. Finally, the brain directs the appropriate body parts to respond quickly enough to avoid any danger.

All of this brain activity must happen in seconds when we drive. We know this is beyond the capability of people who are sleepy, under the influence of certain medications, alcohol or drugs.[53] It is also beyond the capability of people whose brains are damaged by trauma, illness, stroke, or dementia.

For example, if a ball rolls in front of your car, you stop because you expect a child to run out into the street, chasing the ball. Someone with difficulties in executive function may not stop until he sees the child in the street. Even at 20 miles an hour, this may be too late. The impaired driver may see the child and not understand how to respond, or she may not be able to coordinate moving her foot from the gas pedal to the brake in time. The result is tragedy!

Executive function usually deteriorates before other brain functions. Mom may know who and where she is and she could still have problems with executive function. Even if an impaired senior has not had accidents yet, there is no way to predict how the dementia will progress over time. These seniors cannot say, "Watch out! Tomorrow, I won't be able to drive safely." We usually find out after the accident, when it is too late.

We do not want to impose unnecessary limits on independent mobility, but neither do we want to create dangerous situations for seniors, or for the community. Testing is important.

Assessing Driving Safety

Departments of motor vehicles in many states have policies for evaluating senior driving. Unfortunately, these tests usually fail to examine executive function and people who should not drive may stay on the road.

Rehabilitation centers offer comprehensive driving assessments to test driving safety. Occupational therapists test vision and hearing, brain function, attention, reaction time and mobility. Many programs also offer monitored driving tests behind the wheel. The results do not just revoke licenses. These tests can also recommend special mirrors, or other adaptations to make driving safer. As of January 2006, the cost of these programs may be covered by Medicare and other health insurance under occupational therapy billing codes.

Senior service organizations and motor clubs also offer driving safety courses. The American Association of Retired Persons (AARP) offers the Driver Safety Program (1-888-227-7669). The American Medical Association (AMA) developed a program to help doctors assess driving safety. This resource includes information about testing and recommendations on finding alternate transportation resources. (See Resources)

If the tests show a driver is unsafe, caregivers must be prepared to disable, or remove the car. Determined drivers may not care that their auto insurance is cancelled, or that their driver's licenses are revoked. In my experience, these drivers **always** have an extra set of keys. Families should tell friends, mechanics and bankers about the situation, so no one helps the senior get access to a car. Local eldercare resources can help caregivers find alternate means of transportation for the senior.

Mom Shouldn't Live Alone Anymore.

One of the most challenging problems for caregivers is an older adult who needs help, but insists she is independent.

****

Mrs. L had been active all of her life, but over the past few weeks, her legs began to swell and she became more short of breath. Her family tried to get her to call the doctor, but she refused.

One day, Mrs. L didn't answer the doorbell and her daughter let herself in with a key. She found Mrs. L sitting on her sofa, breathing rapidly with her entire body severely swollen. In the hospital, Mrs. L was found to have congestive heart failure and pneumonia. She spent several days in intensive care before she embarked on a slow recovery. There were weeks of tests and treatments. Eventually she was able to sit up in a chair.

The doctors advised Mrs. L to enter a skilled nursing facility for rehabilitation, but Mrs. L insisted on going back into her own home alone. Even though she could barely feed herself, she refused to discuss moving in with one of her children. She refused to hire 24-hour help because she "wasn't going to pay money to have a stranger in my house." Mrs. L was examined by the mental health team, but there was no evidence that she was confused or depressed. She was simply unwilling to accept any change in her lifestyle.

Mrs. L and her adult children met with the medical team several times. Everyone understood Mrs. L's wishes were unreasonable, except Mrs. L. Her family presented her with two options: Mrs. L could either move in with her daughter, have daytime nursing and physical therapy and rotating evening and weekend support from her other children, or she could go into a nursing home. There were no other choices. Mrs. L was very angry, but she chose the less restrictive option, her daughter's home.

****

Communication for Cooperation = R-E-S-P-E-C-T

There are several strategies for doing what needs to be done in the face of a senior's refusal. The first step is a geriatric assessment of brain function and physical function. The key issue is whether or not the senior has the right to refuse. Seniors have the right to make bad decisions if they are mentally capable, but they have to be in a position to take the consequences of those decisions.

Even if a legal document says the senior is not capable, you cannot hold up the piece of paper and say, "this means you have to get dressed now." You have to convince the senior to cooperate.

The current generation of seniors survived the Great Depression. They stormed the beaches at Normandy and they survived the Holocaust. They created the post-World War II economic boom and they shouldered the Civil Rights Movement. Today, Rev. Dr. Martin Luther King, Jr. would be 78 years old. President John F. Kennedy would be almost 90. That's who these people are and they do not take kindly to feeling powerless. They are used to tackling obstacles and they will not hesitate to fight just because **you** are the current obstacle! Here are some basic rules:

Pick Your Battles.

Don't fight over things that don't matter. If seniors want to sleep on the floor, cover them up. If they want to shake hot sauce on pancakes, be happy they're eating. As long as what seniors want is not dangerous to them, or someone else, caregivers should honor seniors' choices. This may be inconvenient, or disruptive to your schedule and sometimes it will upset your sensibilities. You should not have to rearrange every minute of your life, but when you can, as much as you can, give in.

Give Them as Many Choices as Possible.

Does she want to wear the green shirt, or the blue one? Does he want toast, or a bagel? Does she want to do this first, or that first? Keep to the schedule of his favorite TV shows, activities and routines as much as possible. Does the bath have to happen now, or can we do it after Wheel of Fortune? All of the options you offer should be equally safe and acceptable. Give her the choice, but...

Don't Give Them Choices They Can't Really Have.

Don't ask if he wants to go to adult day care when staying home alone isn't safe, there's no money for hired help and you can't take more time off from work. Go out to breakfast, or a store, end up at the adult day care center and let the staff handle the fall-out. The staff can often entice the older adult by recognizing a skill and putting the senior in a position of "responsibility." You can also sweeten the pot with activities the senior wants to do. "This morning, we will go to the center and tonight we will...(favorite activity)."

Older adults may feel threatened by a hired caregiver. A stranger is entering their domain and trying to take over! You may be able to soothe seniors' feelings by saying, "Mrs. Helper is coming today to help with the housework. Here is a list of other things I thought she should do. Did I miss anything? Do you have any other instructions for her?" You may have to give Mrs. Helper a key. Be sure of yourself. Present the schedule with confidence and do not waver, but...

Watch Your Tone of Voice.

Although you may have to make hard decisions and implement them over your seniors' objections, there is no role reversal. No matter how disabled they become, your parents never become your children; they are always your parents. Your tone of voice should be respectful, never abrupt and never patronizing.

Even when my mother no longer recognized me, if I was impatient, or if I spoke too sharply, she would slap me just as fast as she would have done when I was a kid. Just as in marriage, or any other intimate relationship, in eldercare, what you say is often less important than how you say it. Calm, respectful tones are key. Don't argue or contradict, because...

Sometimes, You Gotta Do What You Gotta Do.

You may have to agree in words. Say "yes sir," and go on to do what you need to do. This may work for hiring people, rearranging the house and buying things. It will not work for bathing, dressing and other direct personal care. Here, enticements are the key.

You will probably never hear your senior say, "you know, hiring this respite worker was really a great idea." If you have had a geriatric assessment, you know what needs to be done. If you have worked with a geriatric care manager, or another social service advisor, you know how to do it. Don't argue or plead. Be confident. You're right. It has to be this way. Go on and get it done.

Making the tough decisions in the face of your senior's objections can be uncomfortable, even painful. Make sure you have done your homework and be sure you have enough support. Pick your battles, give appropriate choices and keep to your senior's routine as much as possible. Hear with big-girl (adult) ears, giving honor and respect, but not always obedience.

CHAPTER 7: THE NURSING HOME DECISION

"Never:" Honoring the *Spirit* of the Promise

Recall Mrs. F and her two daughters in Chapter 4. The daughters refused nursing home care until a fall injured all three of them. They had promised never to put Mrs. F in a nursing home. The **spirit** of that promise was that they would always give her the best care. Sometimes, giving the best care means not doing the care yourself.

Many families try to cover 24 hours of care with only one or two people. They assume the responsibilities that require three shifts of nurses and aides in a nursing home. Unlike family caregivers, the nursing home staff goes home after 8 hours! When families insist on this kind of schedule, the quality of care has to suffer. Is this keeping the spirit of the promise?

Choose the Best of Bad Options.

Many families think seniors get worse in nursing homes and, if people die shortly after being admitted, families think the nursing home killed their loved one. Neither situation is true.

Patients with memory loss function by relying on cues in an environment that has not changed since their brains were healthy. Their memory and function only appear to get worse in unfamiliar surroundings. Without familiar cues, these people cannot compensate, or cover the depth of their memory loss. They were actually that sick at home; they only appear to get worse in the nursing home.

People who have to live in nursing homes are not healthy people. They cannot take care of themselves because of serious chronic conditions that are not expected to improve. In my experience, families use the nursing home too late. They wait until the senior's illness is so advanced, or the caregiver is so tired, ill, or injured that it is impossible to provide the proper care at home. By the time loved ones are admitted into the nursing home, their health is poor at best. Then, seniors do what their chronic illnesses dictate; they get worse and they die.

In nursing homes, the nursing staff handles the day-to-day care and families monitor the care. This arrangement allows families to spend the remaining time doing things **with** and **for** their loved ones, not **to** them. It also allows families to concentrate on advocating for their senior.

Stay in Control of the Care Plan.

You are still the caregiver when your senior is in the nursing home. You do not give up the rights, nor the responsibilities of being your senior's primary advocate. Your senior's best interests are served when you understand how to get the information you need and how to voice your concerns effectively.

Make the Other Families Your Allies

Families of nursing home patients can join forces to increase resources in advocating for loved ones.

****

Mrs. K and Mrs. P had been roommates in the nursing home for more than a year. When Mrs. K's daughter came to visit, she would see Mrs. P playing bingo in the hall and she would get a full report from Mrs. P about her mom. Mrs. P laughed, "she's up there telling jokes and running things," or sometimes Mrs. P looked worried and she reported, "she's not feeling well today." The two families chatted often when they ran into each other on visits.

At one point, the nursing assistants assigned to Mrs. P and Mrs. K commented that Mrs. P seemed more irritable; she was less interested in playing bingo. They also informed the registered nurse (RN) that Mrs. P soiled her underpants and hid them in the bathroom. The staff seemed to think Mrs. P's illness was "just getting worse." (See Chapter 2: Don't Deny-Agism)

A couple of weeks later, the nursing home administrator called Mrs. K's daughter to tell her that Mrs. K would be switching rooms. The administrator said Mrs. P had become verbally abusive to Mrs. K and they were separating the ladies for safety reasons.

Mrs. K's daughter was concerned----about Mrs. P. The change in behavior was not consistent with the relationship between the two roommates. Mrs. K's daughter contacted Mrs. P's daughter.

Mrs. P's family discussed the changes in her behavior with the RN and with her doctor. After examining Mrs. P, the doctor admitted her to the hospital with a severe urinary tract infection. Mrs. P was treated with a course of antibiotics and, after a few days, she returned to the nursing home and her roommate.

****

Get to Know the Nursing Home Staff.

The certified nursing assistants (CNAs) and the aides who are assigned to care for your senior are the best source of information on the residents' daily life. The aides and CNAs should know whether or not Dad is eating, how he participates in activities and how he gets along with other residents. The aides should know whether Mom needs any toiletries, clothing, or supplies.

The RN on the floor will know about medications and any changes in health status. The RN should be your first contact about any concerns or complaints.

Talk to the staff. This is not just a ploy; it is a way to develop relationships to make the environment more pleasant for you, for the staff and for your loved one. Also, you can get clear impressions about the environment in the facility from the security guards, receptionists, dietary and housekeeping staff. You should not expect these workers to be spies or informants, but informal, casual conversations can give you impressions about your loved one's quality of life in the facility. This information can either ease your mind, or let you know it is time to make a change.

Attend the Quarterly Care Conferences.

Nursing homes are mandated to review residents' care plans at least every three months. Families must be notified of the conference time in advance. You can reschedule the conference to a more convenient time for you, but prepare to be flexible. Bring a list of questions or concerns. You may also bring an advocate with you (another family member, clergy, or a geriatric care manager) and you may take notes. Be sure to ask how problems will be resolved, how solutions will be monitored, when you should expect to hear the results and which staff member will communicate with you.

Inform the Administration About Serious or Repeated Problems.

If your concerns are not addressed by the nursing staff on the floor, you should contact the director of nursing, or the nursing home administrator. If the problem involves a health issue or a medication, you should contact the doctor's office. Leaving messages at the nursing home may not be an effective way to communicate with the doctor. (See Chapter 2: The Physician User's Manual)

Contact the Ombudsman

Most states offer a program to address issues of elder abuse and neglect as well as other serious problems in the nursing home. An ombudsman is not a nursing home employee. The ombudsman is an independent investigator and mediator. Most ombudsmen are trained by departments on aging to work with nursing home administrators, residents and families. They look into allegations of mistreatment, hazards and safety violations. The nursing home will have contact information for the ombudsman assigned to the facility, but you can find this information independently, through the department on aging, or the area agency on aging.

Don't Just Be a Squeaky Wheel.

Of course, you should raise your concerns, but people will become insensitive to your needs if you only complain. Be professional and courteous at all times. Sarcasm and condescension are just as bad as yelling and cursing. **You** will be noticed, but your concerns will be overshadowed and minimized.

Participate in holiday celebrations and special programs. Attend support groups and educational seminars. The activity department is always open to stimulating entertainment for residents and education for staff. Bring your talents to the nursing facility. Most activity departments will gladly schedule your choirs, dance troupes, plays, crafts and just about anything else to bring a smile to the residents.

If you have a specific skill, offer to give a seminar for staff, families, or residents. Discussions about topics of general interest can usually be incorporated into programs for staff development or family education.

I think of nursing homes as powerful medications that may have great benefits as well as negative side effects. Families must learn how to access the benefits and decrease the risks by recognizing their own limitations. Caregivers should also become effective advocates for their loved ones. In this way, families honor the *spirit* of the promise to **always give the best care.**

CHAPTER 8: END OF LIFE CARE

Add Life to Years, Rather Than Years to Life

Hospice care is designed to provide comfort and dignity to people with incurable illnesses. This supportive program also helps caregivers through their loved one's illness. Hospice continues to support families through the grieving process after the loved one has passed on. One would think that suffering families would rush to participate in such a wonderful service, but hospice care is woefully under-utilized.

Hospice professionals agree that only about 1/3 of the people who are eligible for hospice services actually enroll in the program. Most of these people enter hospice care only in the last three days of life.

My family enjoyed the support and the services of the hospice program for six months. Why were we so lucky when so many other families miss this opportunity? I believe we were able to take full advantage of the hospice program, because we did not deny that Mother was dying. We were able to face her transition, because our family did not function under three fallacies many people cling to:

- **Death is optional.**
- **Technology is God.**
- **Death is failure.**

Death is Not Optional.

Between 1947, when penicillin became widely available and 1984, when the threat of AIDS was widely recognized, Americans lived in the era of **Cure**. In these years, medical science developed increasingly potent antibiotics and cancer chemotherapy. Doctors snatched people from the jaws of death with cardiopulmonary resuscitation (CPR), ventilators (breathing machines), kidney dialysis and by transplanting almost every organ. Today's older adults, most of their caregivers and most practicing health care professionals have lived through these years of **Cure**. Everyone has come to expect medical miracles.

Many healthcare dollars are spent in the last weeks of life, using invasive, futile and sometimes abusive technology in vain attempts to save people from terminal illnesses. Are we so intoxicated with the technology that we fail to consider the outcome?

Between the ancient era of the pharaohs and 1947, the world was in the age of **Care**; cure was rarely possible. The healthcare system may be headed backwards. Since the 1980s, AIDS, the emergence of other infections that are resistant to common antibiotics, West Nile virus, Ebola virus, Severe Acute Respiratory Syndrome (SARS), avian flu and other new infections threaten to put us back into the era of **Care**. This shift will not occur because we lack the technology. Medical professionals will still be able to perform dramatic procedures, but we may be unable to cure the infections that often follow. We will have to give up the illusion that death is optional.

Technology is Not God.

Dr. Bernie Siegel is a Harvard cancer surgeon who has written a series of moving books including, <u>Love, Medicine and Miracles</u>.(54) He tells us many patients die quickly, even if their illnesses are supposed to respond to treatment. Other patients carry dismal diagnoses, yet they outlive their doctors. Technology does not have all of the answers.

We should embrace medical science enthusiastically when it can provide information to cure, prevent illness, or relieve suffering. Technology becomes irrelevant when it can neither comfort, nor change the condition that causes death. No matter how exciting aggressive therapies appear, they are just procedures, like setting a broken limb, or operating to remove an infected appendix. Procedures have indications and contraindications, reasons to use them and situations in which they should not be used either because they show no benefit, or because they cause harm. A doctor would not amputate a leg to treat pneumonia, so why would she use cardiopulmonary resuscitation (CPR) to treat widespread cancer?

CPR was developed in the 1960s to treat sudden, abnormal heart rhythms in people whose hearts had the capacity to heal.(55) The best outcome of CPR occurs when the rhythm changes are seen on heart monitors, by professionals, in intensive care units. Then, machines and medications are used to support the patient until the heart heals. CPR was never intended to treat conditions where the heart is not the main problem, or where the heart is too damaged to heal.(56)

Four questions should be asked when any treatment is considered:

- Was the procedure designed for this situation?

- How likely is the procedure to meet its goal compared to the amount of discomfort it may cause?

- If the procedure meets its goal, will this change the primary cause of dying?

- If the procedure will not change the cause of dying, will it increase comfort?

****

Mrs. C has end-stage heart failure and anemia (a low blood count). One possible cause of anemia in a woman her age is slow bleeding in her bowels, possibly from a cancer. Mrs. C's heart is so damaged that she cannot tolerate the stress of surgery. Her family and doctors are faced with a decision. Should they perform a procedure to see if Mrs. C has a cancer in her bowel? The procedure is relatively simple to perform, but it is uncomfortable and there is some risk of bleeding, or poking a hole through the bowel. Even if the doctors find a cancer, Mrs. C's heart is too weak to survive surgery to remove it. Her family decided it made no sense to perform the procedure.

****

I think Mrs. C's family made the right decision. Why draw a map to a place you can't go? Why impose even a little discomfort, or risk to get information you cannot use?

I have often refused to authorize a procedure when it was ordered "just to know." When information will not cure, or ease suffering, I am perfectly willing to get the information when procedures cannot hurt the person at all, at an autopsy.

Death is Not Failure.

Many families believe they have failed their loved one if they do not use every available bit of technology. If a loved one stops eating because of terminal brain failure such as Alzheimer's disease, is it appropriate to put a feeding tube into his stomach? We have the technology to improve hydration and nutrition, but doing this will not stop the illness. The loved one is dying from Alzheimer's disease, not dehydration, or malnutrition. In this situation, a feeding tube will only make sure that it takes longer for the loved one to die. We often extend life long enough for the patient to develop more difficult problems, like pressure sores (bed sores) and infections. Is this the right thing to do?

Families can be so distracted by the technology that they fail to see death coming. They just keep looking for the next possible procedure. Even if the procedures are simple, they may not be appropriate to the situation. Instead of looking down at each step, families should look ahead to see that they are walking their loved one down the best road. The destination is the same; death is coming. The cost of being on the wrong road is paid in your loved one's suffering.

Doctors are in a position to introduce families to hospice care, but many doctors also see failure in not "doing everything." The explosion in technology has made the "bells and whistles" seem more "doctorly" than words of encouragement and comfort care. We doctors pride ourselves on assessing a patient's condition and recommending the most beneficial treatment course, without exposing the person to unnecessary risk. Many of us forget this principle at the end of life, when we order treatments that are technically possible, but have no hope of cure, improvement, or comfort. Technology usually prolongs suffering in people who have come to the last stages of chronic disease. In these situations, someone should scream, **"Don't just do something! Stand there!"**

Why Are We Doing This?

It is important to know who you're doing this for. Some people are emotionally dependent on the dying family member and they can not bear to be without her. These people prolong the person's dying and suffering so they, themselves, won't be alone. Again, when you do this for yourself, the cost is paid by your loved one.

Some families believe choosing to say "no" to inappropriate technology at the end of life constitutes "playing God by just letting people die." God does not need a ventilator. Neither does He need doctors to hold on to people until He gets back from lunch. It is supremely arrogant to presume that our technology alone has the power to overcome death. When families insist on "doing everything," to stop people from dying, who's trying to play God?

There is a Better Way

The term we use to refuse useless technology may be a barrier to humane end-of-life care. Do Not Resuscitate (DNR), is an order given so CPR will not be used and patients will not be kept alive on breathing machines. The term DNR makes families focus on what they will **not** do. Comfort care focuses on what we **will** do to care for the person. Doctors describe useless end-of-life procedures like CPR as **"do nots"** (DNR) and families may assume they are failing to do something helpful. Instead, doctors can recommend that families **"do"** comfort care when it is appropriate. I often tell families "instead of doing **that** (CPR, or other high-tech procedures that are no longer appropriate), we can do **this** (comfort care, pain control, other physical comforts and dignity)." No one has given up; everyone is still actively giving appropriate care.

Recently, I heard a comforting term that may be more acceptable to families and doctors. "Allow Natural Death" (AND) (57), focuses on what we **do**, rather than what we **do not**. If the medical profession adopts the term "AND," everyone may feel better about choosing the comfort care course when appropriate.

Advance Directives: How Do You Want to Live?

The best way to insure that the end- of- life *is* the last step in living well is to give everyone directions in advance. Advance directives help families to avoid making difficult decisions when they are highly emotional and consumed with grief. Advance directives relieve the guilt and fear of making the wrong decision. These documents also help to avoid rifts between family members that might be felt for generations to come.

****

A young woman had been disabled for many years and she could not communicate well enough to make her wishes known. Her husband wanted to withdraw a feeding tube and her parents went to court to prevent this. Politicians, entertainers and national clergy weighed in on both sides of this argument in a public debate over this family's painful and very personal struggle.

****

I have been at many bedsides where families were fighting instead of hugging and praying together. The fighting could have been avoided if the person in the sickbed had executed an advance directive, to inform everyone whom he trusted to make health care decisions on his behalf and what he would consider a reasonable quality of life. The family might disagree on the plan, but they know "this is what Daddy wanted." They are less likely to attack each other and ruin the legacy Daddy lived to create. If he dies while the family is in an uproar, will there still be happy Thanksgiving dinners? Probably not.

No one expects to be disabled, but we cannot always avoid disability. Make life easier for the people who will take care of you. While you are still healthy, prepare a document that designates someone (Agent) to carry out your wishes. This person will speak for you if you become mentally, or physically disabled, or if you are otherwise unable to speak for yourself. Choose someone whom you trust to follow your wishes, not their own. The document should also describe the kinds of decisions you want your agent to make. For example, if you can not breathe or eat on your own, will you want to be kept alive on machines? What other procedures are important to you? What procedures will you definitely want to avoid?

The most common documents are the **Living Will** and the **Durable Power of Attorney for Health Care.** Living Wills are activated only in the event of terminal illness and they give very specific directions, for example, "if I am too sick to speak with you myself and I am dying, do A, B and C, but don't do D, E, or F."

The Living Will applies only if you are sick enough to die. If your illness is reversible, or if the illness will not cause death, the Living Will has no meaning. The Living Will is equally ineffective if you give the directions about "A to F" and "G" happens. A Durable Power of Attorney for Health Care is much more flexible. This document allows you to choose a person who knows you, someone you trust, to deal with any situation the way you would if you could.

Advance Directives do not lock you in, or limit your choices; they insure that your choices are respected even when you cannot voice them yourself. You can change or revoke your advance directive at any time. Even if you are sick, your wishes will override the document as long as you can demonstrate that you understand your options and the consequences of each path. You can talk, write, blink, nod, gesture, or communicate in any other way. The Advance Directive does not apply as long as you can demonstrate that you understand.

Most states do not require a lawyer to prepare health care advance directives. Forms are available from hospitals, home health agencies, senior centers and area agencies on aging. Some doctors' offices also have forms. Most people will not need both a living will and a power of attorney for health care, but if you travel frequently, both documents may be useful. You need to find out if the state, or the country you plan to visit recognizes one, or both of the advance directive documents from your state. Give photocopies of the document to your doctor and any other interested people, but sign at least three copies. Your copy should have an original signature, as should the documents you give to your agent and your attorney. I learned this hard lesson when I tried to access my mother's safe deposit box during her illness. The bank would not allow me to open the box because the signature on my power of attorney document was photocopied. The document with an original signature was in the safe deposit box!

Many people believe a spouse automatically has power of attorney, but a marriage license is not a power of attorney. While recognizing next of kin is a convention, it is not a legal status. If your spouse makes a decision and any other adult family member disagrees, that person can initiate a court battle, no matter how distant the relationship. Your spouse will probably win the legal battle eventually, but the process can delay decisions that might be critical to your health.

Some people believe the executor of a will has automatic power of attorney for health care. This is not true. Wills outline directions for handling your affairs after you die. When it comes to health care decisions, it doesn't matter if you die; it matters if you don't. Advance directives are less about dying than they are about how you want to live.

No one can predict disability! **Everyone** should give written permission for **someone** to make health care decisions in the event of a serious illness. Do not wait until you are unable to participate in your care plan; then it is too late to give this permission to someone you trust.

Most people do not choose an advocate and they become disabled with no one to speak for them. Healthcare surrogacy laws allow family members, or two physicians to make decisions in a life-threatening emergency when there is no legal advocate. Unfortunately, the ill person does not have control of which family members and which doctors control her life. Stay in control. Choose your advocate in advance.

Hospice: "...To Transform Dying into the Last Act of Living Well" *Motto of the VITAS Hospice Charitable Fund*

Most families believe hospice care is cancer care, but families who face any terminal illness can benefit from hospice. End-stage Alzheimer's disease and other dementias, stroke, Parkinson's disease, end stage heart, lung, liver and kidney disease are all hospice appropriate illnesses.

Many families and their doctors believe patients must be very near death to enroll in hospice and they wait until their loved one's last days before considering hospice care. These patients and families miss weeks or months of supportive care they could have received by working with a hospice team earlier.

A terminal illness is required for hospice enrollment. By convention, hospice estimates a life expectancy of less than six months, but we have already discussed how inaccurate these predictions can be. I believe an illness is terminal when medical science cannot stop it from claiming a person's life. The designation "terminal" is not just an estimate of how much time is left. It is also a determination of whether or not treatment will cure, or improve the condition. The hospice option requires a decision about whether dramatic technologies are likely to prolong life, or prolong dying.

Hospice is a philosophy of care, not a location. Patients and families can enroll in the program at home, in a hospital, in a special hospice unit, or in a nursing home. The families that choose hospice care understand that they are not going to win the game so they change the rules. Since **cure** is not possible, these families and their doctors focus on **care.**

Some families feel guilty about enrolling their loved ones in hospice because they think it means giving up and doing nothing. This could not be further from the truth. Hospice care is very active. It involves doctors, nurses, aides, social workers, clergy and volunteers. The hospice team works with families to treat pain, ease breathing and improve the quality of life for a person with a terminal illness.

Hospice supports families from the diagnosis of the terminal illness, through death and beyond. The hospice team usually follows the family for about a year after the loved one dies, to help with the grieving process.

Not Intensive Care, but Intensively Caring

The hospice care team is very active, but team members do not do anything **to** your loved one that will not do something **for** her. Instead of doing painful, invasive procedures that still will not stop the cancer, cure the heart failure, or keep the illness from claiming your family member, hospice offers pleasure, comfort, support, dignity and love. My family had two wonderful experiences with hospice.

My uncle was called "the Deacon" or "Deak" by his childhood friends, because my grandparents made him spend so much time in church; the name stuck with him throughout his life. Uncle Deak ended his journey with prostate cancer in hospice care. Like many patients with terminal cancer, my uncle no longer wanted to eat. Food is love in our family, as it is in many other families and my aunts were frustrated that my uncle could only taste the favorite foods they prepared for him with such love.

Uncle Deak was a jazz fan; instead of forcing him to eat, the hospice team advised my aunts to bring tapes of his favorite artists. Uncle Deak was able to enjoy the music and reminisce with friends and family about good times the music recalled for him. He slipped away to the sounds he loved.

****

In March 2003, it became clear that Mother was entering the last phase of her ten year battle with Alzheimer's disease; further testing could not change her future. My family enrolled her in hospice and immediately, we were wrapped in the warm blanket that is VITAS Innovative Hospice Care, Inc. It was not the Intensive Care Unit, but it was intensive care. The nurse, the aide, the social worker and the pastor saw Mother and they spoke with me several times each week. When Mother's time drew near, she went into "Crisis Care" and an aide was with us around the clock for the last 18 hours. The aide stayed in the background, but she responded quickly when any need arose. She kept Mother's mouth moist and she provided other care to keep Mother comfortable. When I knelt at Mother's side, the aide gave me a pillow to kneel on saying "without this, you won't be able to stay down there as long as you want to."

Nearby family members came to say goodbye and others called from around the country so Mother could hear loving voices wish her a good journey. I lifted my head off of Mother's chest a moment before she took her last breath. I was singing "Swing Low Sweet Chariot." Mother stepped on the chariot and left the planet. It was the most peaceful and beautiful Homegoing I have ever been honored to witness.

Mother slipped into eternity without panic, poking, or prodding and we all had time to say goodbye. We were able to love her…to death. That's what hospice is.

****

CHAPTER 9: WE DEAL WITH GRIEF

Grief Begins Long Before Your Loved One Passes On

Long before seniors die, they grieve the loss of their independence and you grieve it for them. This is "living grief."

****

Mr. and Mrs. McD had a circle of friends with whom they went bowling, played cards, enjoyed plays, movies and restaurants over the 55 years of their marriage. Mrs. McD suffered a series of strokes. Initially, the group tried to involve her in their usual activities, but with each stroke she became less able to participate. Mrs. McD could not follow the strategy of card games and she could not remember how to compute bowling scores. She was puzzled by the simplest questions. Eventually, Mrs. McD could not follow the conversation and she spent many of the evenings staring off into space. The friends began to visit less frequently. They found reasons to exclude Mrs. McD from their outings when she forgot their names and lost control of her bladder.

The friends continued to invite Mr. McD, but he insisted on bringing his wife. He was upset with his friends because they did not try to interact with Mrs. McD and he was very vocal in his anger. The friends eventually stopped calling and Mr. McD became more isolated. Mrs. McD's condition declined until she did not recognize her husband. Mrs. McD's withdrawal left her husband sullen and tearful.

****

Part of Mr. McD's anger was grief that his wife lost the support and stimulation of her relationships. He felt she deserved better after all the years of friendship, but Mr. McD did not understand that his friends were grieving, too. Mr. McD and his friends suffered living grief. They watched part of their group fade away. They lost a part of their world and they did not know how to handle Mrs. McD's illness. The friends were embarrassed and probably a little frightened for her future and for their own futures. This is anticipatory grief, grieving for what is yet to come.

Most seniors and their families experience both kinds of grief. Grandpa's arthritis is so bad that he can't work on the cars he loves. What will he do now? What will he lose next? Grandma's heart is so weak that she spends less time in her garden. How will she spend her days from now on?

It hurts to watch our loved ones decline. It hurts to watch their world shrink. It hurts to watch their embarrassment and frustration. This hurt is living grief for everyone. We grieve the changes in our senior's body and life, but we also grieve the change in our relationship with the loved one.

****

I watched my mother die of dementia for 10 years. I was married. I had children, an extended family, a church family and a large support base of friends and colleagues. I was an experienced geriatrician and a woman of faith. I thought I was prepared for the changes Mother's illness brought. I thought I was prepared for her death, but I was not prepared to feel so totally abandoned.

In those ten years, I had many questions about my kids. Is it normal for my daughter to be doing this at her age? What should I do when my son does that? I wanted my mommy, but she wasn't really there. I had ten years of living grief; I could see Mother; her body was there, but our relationship was not.

In the last hours of Mother's life, as I knelt at her bedside, I held her hand to my face and I said, "please don't leave me alone here." I had lost Mother long ago; I had so many supportive people in my life and I understood it was best for Mother to move on. Still, in those last moments, I felt like my mommy was going away and leaving me alone for the very first time. I was Dr. Geriatrics of the Planet; I had made all of the big decisions and I had cared for Mother over the years, but that day, I was just a grieving child.

****

There is no role reversal in grieving. Even if your seniors have been dependent on you for years, they are still your seniors. When they are sick, or injured and when they die, you grieve as a child. You are in the double bind of having to be in control and having your foundation crack at the same time. Living grief is a big factor in caregiver stress.

Grieving Dementia, the *"Slow Walk Home"*

Bishop T. D. Jakes

Living grief is more difficult when the illness is dementia. This type of grief is worse for a caregiving spouse than it is for a child.

****

Remember Mr. and Mrs. McD. When their friends withdrew, Mr. McD was increasingly isolated. All of the activities he had enjoyed over the years were for couples. Although he was not yet a widower, he was a single. Mr. McD felt uncomfortable at dinners, going bowling and participating in other activities by himself, but taking Mrs. McD along was painful for everyone.

Mr. McD stopped going out. He spent more time with Mrs. McD, yet that made him feel her loss more intensely. She had not only forgotten their history, she no longer reacted to the funny, intimate gestures they had shared. Mrs. McD could not recall their inside jokes and eventually, she did not even recognize her husband. One minute, she was agitated, thinking he was a stranger who had come to hurt her; the next minute, she held on to him, sobbing. The McDs had been high school sweethearts and they each were the other's soulmate. Mr. McD was devastated by the living grief of watching his wife slip away from him; he lost his soul mate, his life partner and the joy in his life.

****

When people suffer physical illness, the changes are usually visible. The weakness, odors, weight loss, swelling, or signs of pain remind caregivers that the loved one **has** changed. Many people with dementia are physically healthy for a long time. They usually look like themselves until very late in the illness and caregivers can forget the relationship has, indeed changed. Your emotions reach for a response that will never be there again and you feel this pain every……single…… time---every time you come into the house, every time you come into the room, every time you turn around. Bishop T.D. Jakes calls dementia the "slow walk home."(58) How can anyone understand the countless little losses spouses suffer when they live with a partner who slowly walks away from more than 50 years of memories?

Grief and Guilt: Wishing it Was Over

Grief is easier to manage when a loved one dies suddenly, because good memories can comfort us. It is much worse when the person deteriorates before our eyes, because reality gets between us and the memories; this leaves little room for comfort. Living grief intensifies as we watch our loved one's physical suffering, his growing dependence and her isolation in the illness. Everyone grieves the loss of relationships. Why wouldn't you want it to be over for them and for you?

Wishing it was over does not mean you want to kill the person. It does not mean you want the person dead so you can be free from caregiving. You wish everyone could be free from the situation. This is neither selfish, nor heartless, nor cruel. Guilt about these feelings only adds another layer of suffering.

I am not a proponent of euthanasia. I believe physical suffering can be eased and emotional suffering can be soothed through hospice care. I do propose that caregivers respect the effects of living grief and factor in these effects when they calculate the stress of caregiving. Caregivers who do not change dressings, perform heavy lifting, or manage complicated medication schedules may believe their caregiving burden is light. These caregivers fail to recognize that they deserve respite and other supports, because they believe they are not doing heavy duty. Grief is also a heavy duty and I urge you to get the support you need, even if your caregiving duties are not very physical.

CHAPTER 10: THE FAILURE OF PUBLIC POLICY

If you are not interested in public policy, you may want to skip this chapter, but I hope you won't. This chapter is intended to help you understand why our current health system fails seniors and their caregivers. Hands-on caregivers are the best eldercare advocates; I hope to arm you with information to make you a more effective advocate for your seniors and for other caregivers. I hope this chapter will also raise questions that you want to investigate further. This information will make your voice more effective as you encourage legislators to make changes to benefit people with chronic illnesses and their caregivers.

Demographics Don't Drive the Dollars.

With the babyboomers entering the senior ranks, one would think senior services would be abundant and affordable. One would think service industries would be eager to support older people who need care. This is not the case. For example, in 2002, the Robert Wood Johnson Foundation completed a survey of adult day care services in the United States. Twenty-three of the fifty states offered less than 30% of the required adult day care services. Only 6 states approached 70% of the need and this group included states that are very small (Rhode Island and New Hampshire) and states that have a relatively small senior population (Alaska and Hawaii).[59]This represents the current adult daycare shortfall. Think about what will happen when the babyboomers need adult day care.

Another congressional report published in 1990 compared state spending for investigations of abuse and neglect among children and seniors. Although the senior population is growing more rapidly, (See Chapter 1 *More* Older Adults) the money spent on elder abuse was less than 10% of the amount spent on child abuse.(60)

Medicare-Paying to Do Things *to* People Not *for* People

Medicare Doesn't Do What You Think It Does.

Medicare was designed in the 1960s when there was little chronic illness. If you became ill, either you recovered completely, or you died. Medical technology has insured that fewer people die of a specific illness, but today many people live long enough to wish they were dead. Even so, Medicare funding has not made the shift from Acute Cure to Chronic Care. Medicare pays for expensive procedures that are expected to cure, but it does nothing to address lost independence from unrelenting, chronic disability.

Medicare pays for procedures and machines, but Medicare does not cover supervision, or supportive services that could keep a senior in the community.

Medicare will not pay for:

- Assistance with medications, shopping, cooking, personal care, or finances

- Transportation, adult day care, or companions

- Housekeeping, or other chore services

The New York Times reported that major universities were forced to close their diabetes education and prevention centers even though the centers successfully educated patients and improved diabetes control. These programs could not afford to stay open. Medicare would not pay even $200 for podiatrists to prevent, or aggressively treat diabetic foot ulcers and prevent an amputation. Medicare was willing to pay over $30,000 for an amputation and all of the associated rehabilitation services! (61)

Medicare has continually decreased payment to doctors despite the increasing number of Medicare recipients. Medicare uses the Sustainable Growth Rate (SGR) formula to determine the rate of payment. Unfortunately, this formula is not based on the actual cost of care, nor does the formula question whether the money is spent wisely. The SGR formula calculates payment rates based on the amount of money the system lost in the previous year. Consultants have recommended a formula that reflects the actual cost of care, but SGR remains in force. If Congress does not adopt a more reasonable approach, Medicare will pay doctors less in 2007 than it paid us in 2001 even though the senior population will be larger. (62)

Doctors and other professional caregivers join family caregivers in taking responsibility for **more** older adults, **older** older adults and **sicker** older adults as the population ages. (See Chapter 1: Aging America) Medicare does not support the work that geriatricians do. (See Chapter 10: Geriatrician's Dilemma: Serve Seniors or Feed Your Children)

Nursing Home Financing

Many caregivers believe Medicare pays for all nursing home care, but state-supported public aid programs, patients and their families are the primary payors. Medicare will make partial payment for about 4 months of care only if the nursing home resident meets strict criteria.

Medicare pays 100% for the first 20 days of a nursing home stay. For the next 100 days, Medicare covers all costs except a $119 per day co-payment from the patient and family. If the patient needs to stay in the nursing home more than 120 days, Medicare pays **nothing**.

Nursing home residents qualify for Medicare support only under these conditions:

- They have a "skilled nursing need," and a treatment plan that requires a registered nurse (RN) to be available 24 hours a day.

- They were hospitalized for three consecutive nights immediately prior to being admitted to the nursing home.

- They are admitted to the nursing home for the same illness that was treated in the hospital.

Physical, occupational and speech therapies, wound care, intravenous medications, or breathing treatments qualify as skilled nursing needs. When a patient cannot benefit from skilled services (like Mrs. F in Chapter 4: Financial Health), or when the care need goes beyond 120 days, families must either pay privately, or apply for public aid. (63)

Medicare will support another 120 days of skilled care only if the patient stays out of the hospital and any other Medicare-supported facility (nursing home or rehabilitation center) for a period of 60 days. Then, there must be another 3-night hospital stay and another skilled nursing need before the 120-day Medicare clock resets.

Families Inherit Seniors' Financial Resources, or Use the Assets to Pay for Care.

When patients need nursing home placement, their finances are carefully reviewed to compute a "spend-down" figure. Patients and their families must pay this amount of money out-of-pocket before the state assumes the cost of nursing home care through public aid. Property, bank accounts and investments, pensions and other financial resources must be liquidated and the funds paid to the nursing home. The spend-down figure includes any assets that were transferred out of the senior's estate in the previous 36 months. The state may also place liens against property, so money from any future sale is earmarked to reimburse public aid.

Many families are upset about liquidating assets instead of inheriting them. They say, "We don't want to give the state all of Daddy's money," but why shouldn't Daddy's resources pay for his care?

What About the Healthy Spouse?

When one spouse needs care and the other one does not, families may worry about having enough money to support the healthy spouse. Public aid programs employ a "spousal impoverishment" policy. This policy reserves a major portion of the disabled senior's assets to support the healthy spouse. The funds can also support a blood relative who served as a live-in caregiver for more than three years. In 2006, the resources are split so the healthy spouse or caregiver's "half" contains one home and its furnishings, one car, burial funds, up to $2,488 in monthly income and up to $99,540 in assets. The remaining funds go toward the "spend-down." Healthy spouses and long-term caregivers retain enough resources to support themselves comfortably.(64)

Medicare does not support the type of care most seniors need and it does not support the people who provide the care.

Where Are the Geriatricians?

The Veterans Administration Medical Centers opened the first geriatric medicine programs in the United States in the 1970s. Since then, hundreds of doctors have trained to care for older adults. Unfortunately, the number of doctors who start in the service of seniors and the number who stay in the service of seniors are both dwindling. Careers in geriatrics are hard to sustain financially. There is very little professional incentive to become a geriatrician and even less financial incentive to work as a geriatrician once a doctor completes the training.

Academic Geriatricians: Researchers, Teachers, Leaders

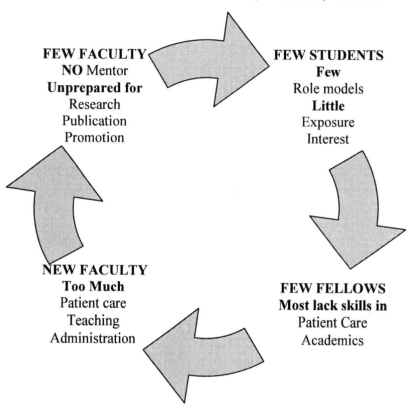

FEW FACULTY
NO Mentor
Unprepared for
Research
Publication
Promotion

FEW STUDENTS
Few
Role models
Little
Exposure
Interest

NEW FACULTY
Too Much
Patient care
Teaching
Administration

FEW FELLOWS
Most lack skills in
Patient Care
Academics

Few geriatrics fellows have the opportunity to develop into successful faculty members so few geriatrics professors are available to serve as role models for students. Without role models, few students choose to enter geriatric fellowship training programs and there are few fellows. This is a cycle that spirals downward, blocking the production of geriatricians.

Medical Students Lack Role Models and Incentives to Study Geriatrics.

The Association of Directors of Geriatric Academic Programs (ADGAP) conducted surveys about training in geriatrics. Most medical schools and residency programs offered geriatrics courses, but these courses were not integral, mandatory parts of the curriculum. No more than 10% of students took advantage of the opportunities. [65, 66]

Most geriatricians begin their training in the primary care specialties, internal medicine and family practice. An increasing number of students shy away from primary care to pursue more procedure-oriented careers, because Medicare and health insurance companies pay more for procedures. The academic geriatrics community suggests that career choices may be driven by the high cost of medical education. Students have huge loans to repay and they may need more money than they can earn in primary care. [67]

Respected role models might encourage students to overlook the financial obstacles, but there are few geriatrics professors. Most of these professors stay in the lower academic ranks as assistant professors and they spend most of their time seeing patients. These professors may not earn the respect, nor wield the power that higher ranking faculty members enjoy. Students are not likely to emulate geriatricians who work like slaves, do not have the respect of the powers that be and whose work is often seen as futile by other respected faculty.[68] (See Chapter7: Death Does Not Equal Failure)

The Geriatrics Fellows' Handicap

Geriatrics fellows begin their training without the basic information, because so little geriatrics is taught in medical school and residency programs. Fellows in other subspecialties have no such handicap. New cardiology fellows learn about heart disease through four years of medical school and three years of residency training. The cardiology fellow does not know how to perform specialized tests, or how to develop new uses for the tests, but she comes into fellowship training with seven years of basic knowledge to build upon.

Most new geriatrics fellows have had little, if any formal teaching about memory loss, mobility, or prescribing the level of care. (See Chapter 2: Level of Care Prescription) Geriatrics is a team sport, yet most new fellows do not know how to play on the team. They have never worked with the nurses, social workers, pharmacists, nutritionists, rehabilitation and mental health professionals who are essential members of the geriatric evaluation team.

Most medical training occurs in hospitals, but geriatric care is given in many sites. New geriatrics fellows are not prepared to work in patients' homes, in nursing homes, or in assisted-living facilities. Neither do they know how to collaborate with home health agencies and other community-based eldercare partners.

The primary role of geriatric fellowship training is to create researchers, educators and leaders. Fellows learn how to take care of specific patient care problems, but they should also learn the research and publishing skills that lead to academic success. The best fellowship programs also offer courses in public policy, business management and how to teach and mentor students. It is very difficult to teach all of this in a two-year fellowship program.

Geriatrics Fellows Fall Off of the Academic Ladder.

The promotion pathway for most medical subspecialties, begins with newly graduated fellows starting at the lowest rungs of the junior faculty ladder, as lecturers or instructors. Senior faculty members mentor the junior faculty. They supervise the juniors in research projects and they give the younger faculty opportunities to co-author academic papers. In one to three years, the junior faculty members move to the assistant professor level. Eventually, they develop the skills to become independent researchers and authors. After several more years, junior faculty should have enough research experience and enough publications to earn promotion to the higher academic ranks.

Only a small number of geriatrics fellows graduate each year and if a medical school is committed to developing a geriatrics program, it faces strong competition for faculty applicants. Many schools offer graduating fellows an incentive by appointing them directly into the rank of assistant professor. These new faculty members bypass the lecturer and instructor levels, jumping ahead without the necessary faculty experiences.

These new geriatricians rarely have a senior mentor to advise them, because there are so few geriatrics professors. Junior faculty members in other subspecialties have contracts that protect significant time for research. Most geriatrics professors have no such contract; they spend most of their time taking care of patients and teaching students. This leaves little time for them to conduct research, or publish the journal articles that will push them up the academic ladder.

Some medical schools give new geriatricians responsibility for developing geriatrics programs from scratch. A major university offered me a position as Chief of Geriatrics right after I finished my fellowship; this is not uncommon. Unfortunately, most new graduates lack the necessary management experience for effective program development. They have little time to learn program development skills "on the job," because they work so hard in patient care and teaching.

While it is flattering to be so highly sought after, to have a title and the opportunity to create a new program, graduating geriatrics fellows would do well to remember:

Chief of Nothing Is Nothing!

Department chairpersons and program directors usually compete for financial resources from the dean of the medical school. Even the most talented geriatrics fellow will find it difficult to compete with other chairpersons who are respected senior faculty members. The new geriatrician must contend with experienced researchers who bring money and prestige into the school through research grants and publications. A fancy title does not change this reality.

Geriatricians are crippled as they try to climb the academic ladder, because they have to play "catch-up" to learn the basic geriatrics information. They lack mentors and experience with research and publishing, the keys to academic success. Geriatricians have little time to develop into scholars, because they have overwhelming responsibility for patients, students and program administration.[67] These forces interfere with success in academics, but why are there so few community-based geriatricians?

The Community-Based Geriatricians' Dilemma: Serve Seniors, or Feed Your Children.

We don't have a "geriascope."

Medicare pays for procedures that are designed to cure, but most geriatric illnesses are not curable. Geriatrics is especially vulnerable, because there is no "geriascope." Geriatricians do not have a procedure to charge to insurance companies. Geriatricians **care** even when **cure** is not possible, but health insurance does not support what we do.

The new insurance initiatives that "pay for performance" further threaten the financing of geriatric medicine. Geriatricians care for patients with incurable illness; we will never be successful if Medicare considers patients' declining health and death as evidence of poor physician performance.

Most geriatric patients need more than a 10, or 15 minute office visit. Older adults rarely have just one illness or one medication. There are usually about 3 illnesses and 5 medications. [69] In addition, there are usually complicated social problems that involve caregivers and community services. Doctors need time to evaluate all of the illnesses, to review medications for drug interactions and side effects, to educate patients and caregivers and to coordinate eldercare services. Medicare does not adequately support the extra time, or the expertise in care coordination; other health insurance companies usually follow Medicare's lead.

A practice that serves a predominantly elderly population can go bankrupt, because of rising staff costs, skyrocketing malpractice insurance premiums, increasing numbers of time-intensive Medicare patients and dwindling Medicare reimbursement.

The general public usually thinks Porsche and Mercedes-Benz when doctors say we need more money, but geriatricians have kids with braces and college tuition just like everyone else does. Many doctors are forced to limit the number of Medicare patients they serve, or to stop practicing geriatrics altogether.

Geriatrics Expertise: Invaluable, but Not Valued.

Children are not just little adults and seniors are not simply older versions of younger adults. Like pediatrics, geriatrics is a unique body of knowledge that respects how seniors' bodies work, how they handle medications and how they respond to both disease and treatment.

In 1988, the American Board of Internal Medicine and the American Academy of Family Physicians joined to offer the first Certificate of Added Qualification in Geriatric Medicine (CAQ). This certificate is awarded to geriatricians who study vigorously and successfully complete an examination that takes several hours.

In 1992, the national leaders in geriatrics decided that a doctor could take this certifying examination after completing only one year of fellowship training, instead of two years. The leaders hoped a shorter term would encourage more trainees to choose careers in geriatrics. In 2006, the geriatrics credential was upgraded from a certificate to full sub-specialty status. Neither the shorter training time, nor the higher status has affected the supply of geriatricians. There has been a steady decrease in the number of doctors who demonstrate their commitment to geriatrics by becoming board-certified.

When it came to retaining geriatrics credentials, geriatricians voted with their feet. 2,406 doctors earned the CAQ in the first examination in 1988. Re-certification is required every 10 years, but only about half of these doctors had recertified by 2003. The rest of the geriatricians allowed their credentials to expire.(70) This is completely understandable; board certification does not make any difference in a geriatrician's income. Health insurance companies pay a fully trained geriatrician the same amount that they pay a doctor without specialized training! Certification does not support a doctor's ability to maintain an office, purchase supplies, or maintain the staff needed to serve patients.

It is difficult to develop academic geriatricians who might make groundbreaking discoveries. It is almost impossible to promote and retain geriatrics faculty who might influence students to choose geriatrics careers. It is difficult for a geriatrician to survive financially if she chooses to serve in direct patient care and there is no incentive to maintain cutting-edge skills in geriatric medicine.

The need for eldercare is rising, but there are fewer doctors who practice geriatrics and fewer doctors who know how to practice geriatrics. The shortage of geriatricians threatens the quality of care that will be available to our seniors as their ranks swell.

For This Little Money, Wouldn't YOU Rather Flip Burgers?

A similar problem exists among hired workers who give personal care to seniors. The people who are most directly responsible for eldercare are the least paid, least appreciated and least trained. These factors provide little incentive for workers to choose eldercare.

Nursing home aides and community care workers earn about the same wage as employees working in discount retailers and fast food restaurants, (71) but the work is much more difficult. Aides provide personal care; they groom, bathe, change diapers and feed people who often cannot assist in their own care. Some of the sick people are not very pleasant, either because of illness, or because they are frustrated with their disability. Few personal care workers have health insurance, or other benefits. It is not surprising that job turnover is so high among aides; as soon as these workers can find other employment, they are gone.

Some chains of nursing homes have committed to staff training and in those facilities, some administrators see a decrease in staff turnover. When aides understand why their role is important, they may have more job satisfaction and they may be more committed. Unfortunately, high staff turnover can undermine these training programs. I attempted to implement a training program in a long-term care facility several years ago. Three months after starting the series of seminars, the staff consisted of mostly new people and the training program had to start over. In many facilities, this is a never-ending cycle.

Of course many aides are dedicated, loving eldercare workers, but for others, this is a job of last resort. In some cases, care facilities and community programs are forced to hire people who **can't** work in fast food restaurants. What a frightening thought! In some instances, the people who are most directly responsible for our loved ones may be the **least** capable.

The Myth of Assisted-Living: Planning For People Who Don't Exist

Over the past few years, assisted-living and supportive care facilities have popped up all over the place. Supportive care facilities provide a level of care similar to assisted-living, but supportive care is funded by public aid. Many families see these facilities as life-lines when seniors can no longer live alone. Families think these facilities will meet all of their loved one's needs, allowing caregivers to focus on their jobs and their families without worry. Unfortunately, this is not always the case.

I interviewed an assisted-living facility administrator who insisted that the residents his company served had no major illnesses, "they just need a little help." Administrators and family members have significant incentives to give in to this delusion, but assisted-living programs are designed for people who do not exist. If residents needed "just a little help," they would still be in the community. Either, they need more than a little help, or the help they need cannot be provided by the family, or they have no family to help them.

"WNL:"Within Normal Limits, or We Never Looked?

I have spoken to admissions personnel at assisted-living facilities around the country. Many of these people said they felt financial pressure from their employers to fill the beds—with anybody. They said they feel pressured to bend the rules and admit residents who are really too ill to manage in the assisted-living environment. I do not believe most admissions/administrators have evil motives. Most of them are compassionate people; they want to help caregivers who are at the end of their ropes and they may agree to "give it a try."

In defense of the assisted-living/supportive care industry, the laws that regulate these programs do not allow them to provide medical care, or to admit patients who have certain illnesses, like dementia. Most facilities do not have nurses on- site in the evenings, or on weekends. Although doctors come into the facilities to see their own patients, very few assisted-living programs have medical personnel or protocols. These protocols would allow nurses to monitor all residents for conditions that might require more care.

Facilities have not developed these resources, **because people in these facilities are *not* supposed to need care.**

Despite this, many residents do have serious medical conditions. In many cases, the admissions process is not designed to detect these conditions. Admission to assisted-living facilities can be denied if certain conditions (like dementia) are mentioned. Many families will not volunteer the information. Many facility administrators will not ask.

In reviewing patient care in some of these facilities, I found numbers of patients with undiagnosed memory loss. I also found untreated medical conditions that would be simple to treat if they were noticed. WNL means "within normal limits" in usual medical jargon. In some cases, these letters could mean "we never looked."

****

The staff of one facility thought a patient complained all the time "to get attention." Actually, his hands showed the classic deformity of rheumatoid arthritis with swollen, red, hot joints. **He was in pain!** Simple oral medications relieved his suffering and stopped his "attention-seeking." Unfortunately, the patient also had memory loss; he was not able to communicate his needs effectively.

****

I was asked to see another assisted-living resident to certify that she was capable of managing money (so she could renew her contract with the facility). After assessment, I found that the woman suffered from significant memory loss which had never been documented. The diagnosis caused an administrative uproar. The facility was not at fault. The funding guidelines that govern the program made no provision to screen for memory loss, or to identify advocates (surrogate decision-makers) for residents who are physically capable of living in the facility, but mentally incapable of managing finances. If patients can't sign the contract, they can't stay in the facility. Uh-oh, **empty beds!**

****

One Saturday, I was called to help a resident who had been admitted that week to an assisted-living facility. The woman was found sitting on the floor of her room screaming. She refused to eat or get up. She was transferred to the emergency room of a local hospital where the doctors found no evidence of stroke, medication problems, infection or any other acute illness. The woman had profound memory loss that was not documented on the admission forms, but her family insisted there had been no change; they described her presentation as "Mom's usual forgetfulness." The woman was discharged from the hospital to a nursing home where she could receive the level of care she actually needed.

****

Most Facilities Cannot Recognize Seniors' Care Needs Until It Is Too Late.

Even if residents are totally independent when they are admitted to an assisted-living facility, the risk of disability increases with age. If ongoing monitoring is not built into the system, residents can become inappropriate for the environment with no one being the wiser until a catastrophe strikes. What if a resident develops memory loss after years of living in a facility? If the person becomes confused and wanders out of the building, she could suffer from exposure; she could be mugged, or hit by a car. In most facilities, there is neither periodic medical monitoring to diagnose confusion, nor security that can prevent wandering, because **people in these facilities are *not* supposed to be confused or to wander.**

As it is currently organized and regulated, the assisted-living/supportive care industry is a medical, legal and ethical nightmare waiting to happen. The guidelines do not allow the facilities to monitor the residents. Funding based on empty beds may create a conflict of interest. Administrators assume families will advocate for residents and either continue to access medical care in the community, or through a private physician who comes to the facility. Too often, either there is no family, or the family has breathed a sigh of relief, thinking the facility will take care of everything. Either way, seniors can fall through the cracks.

Many facilities affiliate with home health agencies, or private care services to accommodate patients who are not independent. Families can purchase additional services to help with personal care or medications, but these services are not usually included in the basic assisted-living fees. The additional cost can quickly overwhelm the family budget.

Most facilities offer families the opportunity to purchase medications through a pharmacy that delivers to the facility. Families usually accept this service, because the medications may be less expensive and it is certainly more convenient. Otherwise, the family would have to fill prescriptions at a community pharmacy and deliver the medication themselves.

Most of these pharmacy services monitor for dangerous drug interactions, but many of them do not alert anyone when blood tests are required to monitor the effects of the drugs. Unfortunately, I have seen long-term use of medications that require this monitoring, yet the residents have not had the necessary blood tests for more than a year. Assisted-living regulations do not require these facilities to use pharmacy services capable of performing this type of monitoring.

A Better System

The system can work better to serve the people who actually need it. Comprehensive geriatric assessment and level of care prescriptions should be mandatory prior to admission. Assessments should be updated at regular intervals and whenever the staff or family notices a change in behavior, health, or level of independence. In one facility, I instructed the admissions personnel to perform a widely used mental status examination. They found several applicants with memory loss and they urged these families to have full evaluations before admission. The staff identified several people who were too impaired for the facility. The staff admitted that before the mental status screening started, these applicants would have been accepted for admission.

When residents have illnesses that need more monitoring and supervision, they could be admitted to a specialized area within the facility. There are several wonderful facilities especially designed for residents with memory loss, but even the more general facilities could identify a special wing or floor. This section could have stronger staffing ratios, specific training for staff, special programs for the residents and an appropriate environment to accommodate seniors who wander.

Even when a facility cannot support specialized units, better medical monitoring is possible. Nurse practitioners (NP) or physician assistants (PA) can improve the monitoring and address care needs. The NP or PA can come into the facility for one or two sessions per week to educate staff about signs of deterioration and to address any concerns the staff identifies. The facility does not have to pay the NP or PA. These professionals work in collaboration with physicians; their services can be billed to insurance.

Computer programs exist to flag residents whose medications require routine monitoring. The programs routinely ask doctors about blood tests to monitor the effects of certain medications. The doctors can decide which medications to monitor; they can set the timing of these prompts and decide whether or not the tests are appropriate.

You Are Still the Caregiver.

Until the regulations change, families must be prepared to advocate for their seniors in assisted-living and supportive care facilities. Families must understand that these facilities are **not** nursing homes; they do not have 24-hour nursing personnel. In many facilities, at night, seniors will be as alone as they would be in their own homes.

Do not assume emergency room physicians and hospital staff understand the difference between assisted-living facilities and nursing homes. Most assisted-living residents cannot be readmitted to the facility in the evening, or on a weekend; no nurses are available to carry out any orders requested by the hospital. A family member may have to stay with the senior, or hire a private duty nurse; even a home health agency cannot be available around the clock.

A strong relationship with a primary care physician is as important in assisted-living as it is in any other care site. Whether the doctor comes to the facility, or caregivers accompany the senior to office visits, the family should communicate with the physician regularly to discuss changes in health and function and to review the care plan. (See Chapter 2: Physician User's Manual)

Although families believe assisted-living facilities handle everything, the health and well-being of assisted-living residents depends on the family. Caregivers should have realistic expectations based on understanding what the facilities can and cannot provide. Assisted-living is great at providing activities and socialization, housekeeping, meals and sometimes, medication and transportation. By law, these facilities are not allowed to have the programs or staff to provide **care**. Many facilities have relationships with nursing agencies that provide care services, but these will cost extra.

A Call to Arms: The Legislators Need to Know What You Need.

The 2005 White House Conference on Aging brought together 1,200 of the nations eldercare experts to advise the President and Congress about the needs of older Americans. The conference delegates were the professionals who actually do the work in eldercare; they understand the needs of seniors and the limitations of current eldercare policy. They represented all fields of study and practice: front-line service providers, researchers, educators, public and private sector agency administrators and advocates for family caregivers. If anyone listens, the recommendations will revolutionize eldercare in this country, making eldercare policy more responsive to the needs of 21st Century older Americans, professional caregivers and family caregivers. Unfortunately, there is no evidence that the current political leadership will listen.

The same week that the White House Conference on Aging was held, Congress cut funding for the Geriatric Education Centers (GEC); these programs help to educate the professionals who serve seniors. Eldercare advocates are crying out to reverse past Medicare cuts, to insure proper funding in the future and to shift funds from impossible cure to compassionate care. Today, the cries are falling on deaf ears.

Arm Yourself With Information.

Learn about your state's delegation to the 2005 White House Conference on Aging (www.whcoa.com). Invite a delegate to address your community group and explain the conference process and recommendations. Choose the recommendations that affect you the most and write to your legislators about them. Add personal stories to tell the legislators how your situation would have been different if the recommendations had been in place.

You Can Make the Legislators Listen.

Find out who your local, state and federal legislators are. Find out which legislators serve on committees that handle health care, health care financing, aging, or caregiver issues. Find out how your representatives vote on the issues that concern you. You can find federal legislators on the Internet at www.house.gov or www.senate.gov. Legislators usually have their own websites. You will need to know your full 9 digit zip code to access both of these websites. If you don't know your complete zip code, you can find it on the postal service website www.usps.gov. Each state has a website where you can find information about the state legislators, their committee assignments and their voting records. Your local city or village hall will be able to help you find your local, state and federal representatives.

Tell the legislators your story. Let them know how public policy has affected you. Have you had difficulty finding a doctor, because many of them have stopped participating in the Medicare program? Have you lost time from work because you cannot find affordable adult day care, in-home care, or respite care for your senior? Has your health, your job, your relationship, your finances, or your retirement plans suffered because of caregiving responsibilities?

In an election year, legislators are more likely to attend, or to send representatives to a community forum where constituents can present information. Work with an advocacy group to organize a community legislative forum. The presentations should be as concise and as visual as possible. Personal testimonies and film clips can be very effective. One home health agency took a local congressman on home visits to describe the limitations the agency encounters as they try to care for seniors. The congressman was amazed!

Amplify Your Voice.

Join an organization that advocates for seniors and caregivers. Contact your local or state department on aging, a chapter of AARP, or other advocacy groups. (See Resources) Volunteer with the local, state, or federal agency that addresses an aspect of caregiving that affects you. Join an association that specifically deals with an illness that affects your family. Area agencies on aging, the Alzheimer's Association, the American Heart Association, the American

Cancer Society and other organizations often have community advisory boards that would benefit from your energy.

Get Involved! You CAN Make a Difference!

CONCLUSION

Effective caregivers are physically healthy and they take steps to stay that way. They are not afraid to learn how to get help from health care professionals, from family and friends, from the community and when necessary, from mental health professionals.

Smart caregivers manage their finances and they make sure the resources are in place to care for them as they age. These caregivers insure that their twilight years are truly golden and they are adamant that caregiving responsibilities will not crush their kids.

Responsible caregivers make, document and openly discuss decisions about the conditions under which they would want to live. They formally state their care priorities for the end of life and they designate the people whom they would choose to speak for them if disaster should strike. They realize that doing this is an act of love for their children and other family members.

Strong caregivers understand that they must fill up before they can pour out. They nurture other important relationships to maintain a strong support base. They connect with a larger power to keep their struggles in perspective so that their filling is not wasted, oozing out through cracks of bitterness, disappointment, and "unforgiveness."

Successful caregivers treat themselves to the activities they enjoy and they share their talents with others to strengthen the support base for the entire community.

You are your seniors' most important asset. Remember the instructions that flight attendants give to people who travel with their dependents. In an emergency, **put your mask on first!** The best gift you can give your loved one is a healthy, balanced caregiver. Invest in your senior's primary resource, **YOU!**

You cannot give care, supervise care, or advocate for anyone when you are physically ill, financially strapped, emotionally exhausted, or spiritually bankrupt.

Taking care of you **IS** taking care of them. Carry on!

REFERENCES

1. Federal Interagency Forum on Aging (FIFOA), Older Americans 2004, Key Indicators of Well-being, pg 2.

2. The Honorable Dorcas R. Hardy. "2005 White House Conference on Aging Transcript." 12 Dec. 2005. 9 June 2006 <http://www.whcoa.gov>.

3. National Vital Statistics Report, Vol. 52, No.14, February 18, 2004.

4. National Vital Statistics Report, Vol. 54, No. 14, April 19, 2006.

5. FIFOA, pg 2.

6. Yelena, G. et al. "Trends in Causes of Death Among Older Persons in the US (October 2004)," Bureau of Health and Human Services (BHHS), Center for Disease Control and Prevention (CDC), National Center for Health Statistics (NCHS), April 14, 2006.

7. Yelena.

8. Gregory, S.R. and S.M. Panda. American Association of Retired Persons (AARP) Public Policy Institute, "Women and Long-Term Care Fact Sheet, 2002."

9. National Family Caregivers Association; "Random Sample of Family Caregivers." Summer 2000. (unpublished) 18 July 2006 <http://www.nfcares.org>.

10. Goyer, Amy; "Intergenerational Relationships: Grandparents Raising Grandchildren." American Association of Retired Persons (AARP) Foundation Grandparent Information Center, November 2005. 20 Jan 2006 <http://aarp.org/families/grandparents/>

11. Herbert, L.E. et al. "Alzheimer's Disease in the US Population, Prevalence Estimates Using the 2000 Census." Archives of Neurology. 60 (2003): 1119-1122.

12. "Aging Parents: 5 Warning Signs of Health Problems." 8 July 2006 <http://www.MayoClinic.com>.

13. Gilman, L., "A Doctor in the House: Physicians are reviving a bygone practice to keep tabs on aging patients." Time: Bonus Section Generations, Sunday, 24 Sept 2006. 10 Oct 2006 <http://www.nytimes.com>.

14. The Holy Bible, James 3:4 (KJV).

15. Family Caregiver Alliance 2006 Policy Statement. 8 Sept. 2006 <http://www.caregiver.org>.

16. Cannuscio, C.C. et al. "Reverberations of Family Illness: A Longitudinal Assessment of Informal Caregiving and Mental Health Status in the Nurses Health Study." American Journal of Public Health 92 (2003): 1305-1311.

17. Schulz, R. and S.R. Beach, "Caregiving as a Risk Factor for Mortality: The Caregiver Health Effects Study." Journal of the American Medical Association. (1999):282.

18. National Family Caregivers Association. "Caregiving Statistics: 101 Facts on the Status of Working Women, Professional Women's Foundation." 12 July 2006 <http://www.nfcacares.org>

19. MetLife. "Sons at Work: Balancing Employment and Eldercare." Mature Market Institute, 2003.

20. National Vital Statistics Report. "Deaths: Leading Causes for 2002." (2005):53.

21. National Vital Statistics Report.

22. US Department of Health and Human Services. "Health Consequences of Smoking: A Report of the Surgeon General." 2004.

23. US Department of Health and Human Services.

24. Sears, B. Mastering the Zone: The Next Step in Achieving Super Health and Permanent Fat Loss. New York, NY: Harper Collins, 1997.

25. Greeson, J. It's Not What You're Eating, It's What's Eating You. New York, NY: Pocket Books, 1990.

26. Normandi, C.E. and L. Roark It's Not About Food: Change Your Mind, Change Your Life, End Your Obsession With Food and Weight. New York, NY: Perigree Books, 1998.

27. McGraw, P.M. The Ultimate Weight Loss Solution: The 7 Keys to Weight Loss Freedom. New York, NY: Simon and Schuster, 2005.

28. Smith, R.A., V. Cokkinides and H. J. Eyre. "American Cancer Society Guidelines for Early Detection of Cancer, 2006." CA: Cancer Journal. 56 (2006):11-25.

29. Sambrook, P. and C. Cooper. "Osteoporosis." Lancet 367 (2006):2010-18.

30. Centers for Disease Control and Prevention, Morbidity and Mortality Weekly Report. "Recommended Adult Immunization Schedule—United States October 2005 – September 2006."

31. Block, J.D. and S.C. Bakos. Sex Over 50. Paramus, New Jersey: Reward Books, 1999.

32. Block and Bakos.

33. Wein, A.J. and R.R. Rackley. A Better Understanding of Pathophysiology, Diagnosis and Management. Journal of Urology. 175 (3, Pt 2) (March 2006):5-10.

34. Mitler, M.M., D.F. Dinges and W.C Dement. "Sleep Medicine, Public Policy, and Public Health." Principles and Practice of Sleep Medicine, 2nd ed. Kryger, M.H., T. Roth and W.C. Dement, Ed. Philadelphia, PA: W. B. Saunders Co., 1994. Chapter 14.

35. International Longevity Center USA, Ltd. Policy Report. A National Crisis: The Need for Geriatrics Faculty Training and Development Toward Functional Independence in Old Age. 28 Sept 2001.

36. Zarconi, V.P. "Sleep Hygiene Instructions, Table 52-1." Principles and Practice of Sleep Medicine, 2nd ed. Kryger, M.H., R. Roth and W.C. Dement. Ed. Philadelphia, PA: W. B. Saunders Co., 1994. 545.

37. Zarconi. 545.

38. National Family Caregivers Association and MetLife.

39. Reed, K. "When Elders Lose Their Cents: Financial Abuse of the Elderly." Clinics in Geriatric Medicine. 21 (2005): 365-82.

40. Lantz, M.S. "Elder Abuse: Making A Difference." Clinical Geriatrics 12 (2004): 37-40.

41. Family Caregiver Alliance, Cannuscio and Schultz.

42. Jones, L.B. Jesus in Blue Jeans, A Practical Guide to Everyday Spirituality. New York, NY: Hyperion, 1997. 28-31.

43. Jones. 28-31.

44. Truman, Karol K. Feelings Buried Alive Never Die. 1991 Phoenix, AZ: Olympus Distributing, 2003.

45. Cade, Eleanor. Taking Care of Parents Who Didn't Take Care of You: Making Peace With Aging Parents. Center City, MN: Hazeldon Publishing and Educational Services, 2000.

46. Miller, A. The Drama of the Gifted Child: The Search for the True Self. New York, NY: Basic Books, 1997.

47. Jeffress, R.M. When Forgiveness Doesn't Make Sense. Colorado Springs, CO: Water Brook Press, 2005.

48. Evans, J. "Skills for In-Law Relations, Number One: The Principle of Honor." Marriage on the Rock, God's Design for Your Dream Marriage. 1994. Grand Rapids, MI: Zondervan Corporation, 2005. 267-69.

49. Gibran, K. "On Children," The Prophet. 1923. New York, NY: Alfred Knopf, Inc., 2001. 17-18.

50. The Holy Bible, Exodus 20:12 (KJV).

51. The Holy Bible, Ephesians 6:1 (KJV).

52. "Physician's Guide to Assessing and Counseling Older Drivers" American Medical Association, 2004.

53. Mitler, M.M., D. D. Dinges and W. C. Dement. "Sleep Medicine, Public Policy, and Public Health," Principles and Practices of Sleep Medicine, 2nd ed. Kryger, M.H., T. Roth and W.C. Dement. Ed. Philadelphia, PA: W.B. Saunders, Co. 1994. 455-57.

54. Siegel, Bernie S. Love Medicine & Miracles, Lessons Learned About Self Healing From A Surgeon's Experience with Exceptional Patients. 1986 New York, NY: Harper Collins, 1998.

55. "CPR, Statement of the AdHoc Committee on CPR of the Division of Medical Sciences, National Academy of Sciences, NRC." Journal of the American Medical Association 198 (1966): 372.

56. Coneg, S.P. et al. "Cardiopulmonary Resuscitation in Continuing Care Settings: Time for a Rethink." British Medical Journal 332 (2006): 479-82.

57. Lancaster, J. "Allowing Natural Death." Plain Views. A Publication of the HealthCare Chaplaincy. 13 April 2005. 18 Feb. 2006 <http://www.plainviews.org>.

58. Jakes, T.D. "Never Give Up." audiotape ministry. <http://www.tdjakes.org>.

59. The Adult Day Services Program (with PMD Advisory Services, LLC & Seniors Research Group of Market Strategies, Inc.) "A National Study of Adult Day Services by Partners in Caregiving:" 2002. 26 July 2006 <http://rwjf.org/newsroom/featureDetail.jwp?featureID= 1838pageNum=48type=3>.

60. "Elder Abuse: A Decade of Shame and Inaction." presented by William Benson, National Adult Protective

Services   Association.   23   June   2006.
<http://www.whcoa.gov/about/policy/meetings/summary/
William-Benson-National-Adult-Protective-Services.pdf>.

61. Urbina, I. "In the Treatment of Diabetes, Success Often Does Not Pay." New York Times 11 Jan. 2006. 8 Aug 2006 <http://www.nytimes.com>.

62. Centers for Medicare and Medicaid Services website. Courtesy of Dr. Peter Neale, 24 Aug 2007. <http://www.cms.gov>.

63. "2006 Medicare Costs." Medicare and You. Center for Medicare and Medicaid Services, 2007. 102.

64. "Spousal Impoverishment Resource Eligibility." Section 1924 of the Social Security Act; U.S. Code Reference 42 U.S.C. 1396r-5. 1 Sept 2006 <http://www.cms.hhs.gov/MedicaidEligibility/09_SpousalImpoverishment.asp>.

65. Bragg, E. Association of the Directors of Geriatrics Academic Programs (ADGAP). Email to C. Woodson. 5 July 2006 <http://www.ADGAPstudy.uc.edu>.

66. Bragg.

67. Reuben, D.B. and D.H. Solomon. "Fellowship Training in Geriatrics." American Journal of Medicine 97 (1994): 185-205.

68. International Longevity Center USA, Ltd. Policy Report. A National Crisis: The Need for Geriatrics Faculty Training and Development Toward Functional Independence in Old Age. 28 Sept 2001.

69. Medina-Walpole A. et al. "The Current State of Geriatric Medicine, A National Survey of Fellowship-Trained Geriatricians, 1990 to 1998." Journal of the American Geriatrics Society 50 (2002): 949-55.

70. CDC & Merck Institute of Aging and Health, The State of Aging and Health in America 2004.

71. "ADGAP Longitudinal Study of Training and Practice in Geriatric Medicine." Training & Practice Update 1. 2 (2003).

72. Bureau of Labor Statistics. "Occupational Employment Statistics" 2003. 13 July 2006 <http://www.bls.gov/oes>.

RESOURCES

BOOKS:

Block, Joel D., Susan Crain Bakos, <u>Sex Over 50</u>. Paramus, New Jersey: Reward Books, 1999.

Cade, Eleanor. <u>Taking Care of Parents Who Didn't Take Care of You: Making Peace With Aging Parents</u>. Century City, MN: Hazeldon Publishing and Educational Services, 2000.

Evans, Jimmy. <u>Marriage on the Rock, God's Design for Your Dream Marriage</u>. 1994 Grand Rapids, MI: Zondervan Corporation, 2005.

Gibran, Kahlil, <u>The Prophet</u>. 1923 New York, NY: Alfred Knopf, Inc., 2001.

Greeson, Janice, <u>It's Not What You're Eating, It's What's Eating You</u>. New York, NY: Pocket Books, 1990. (out of print, used copies available).

Jeffress, Robert M. <u>When Forgiveness Doesn't Make Sense</u>, Colorado Springs, CO: Water Brook Press, 2005 (out of print, used copies available).

Jones, Laurie Beth, <u>Jesus in Blue Jeans, A Practical Guide to Everyday Spirituality</u>. New York, NY: Hyperion, 1997.

McGraw, Phillip M. <u>The Ultimate Weight Loss Solution: The 7 Keys to Weight Loss Freedom</u>, New York, NY: Simon and Schuster, 2005.

Miller, Alice. <u>The Drama of the Gifted Child: The Search for the True Self</u>. New York, NY: Basic Books, 1997.

Normandi, Carol Emery and Laurelee Roark. <u>It's Not About Food: Change Your Mind, Change Your Life, End Your Obsession With Food and Weight</u>. New York, NY: Perigree Books, 1998.

Siegel, Bernie. <u>Love, Medicine & Miracles, Lessons Learned About Self Healing From A Surgeon's Experience with Exceptional Patients</u>. 1986 New York, NY: Harper Collins, 1997.

Truman, Karol K. <u>Feelings Buried Alive Never Die</u> 1991 Phoenix, AZ: Olympus Distributing, 2003.

CAREGIVER RESOURCES AND SUPPORT:

Administration on Aging (AoA)

Department of Health & Human Services

<u>Resource Directory for Older People</u>

<www.aoa.gov/eldfam/How_To_Find/ResourceDirectory/resource_directory.asp>

1 (202) 619- 0724

Eldercare Locator 1 (800) 677-1116

Family Caregiver Alliance (See 2006 Policy Statement)

<www.caregiver.org>

1 (800) 445-8107

National Alliance for Caregiving

<www.caregiving.org>

1 (301) 718-8444

National Association of Area Agencies on Aging

<www.n4a.org>

1 (202) 872-0888

Eldercare Locator 1 (800) 677-1116

National Association of Professional Geriatric Care Managers, Inc.

<www.caremanager.org>

1 (520) 881-8808

National Family Caregivers Association

<www.nfcacares.org>

1 (800) 896-3650

A Place for Mom

<www.aplaceformom.com>

1 (877) MOM-DAD9   1 (877) 666-3239

Dutiful Daughters (and Sainted Sons)

<www.dutifuldaughters.com>

1 (770) 552-1504

SeniorBridge

<www.seniorbridge.net>

1 (866) 506-1212

Organizations which promote health, or support research and education about a specific illness may also offer caregiver support programs. For example:

American Association of Retired Persons (AARP)

<www.aarp.org/health> (search "Caregiver Support")

1 (888) OUR AARP

1 (888) 687-2277

AARP Driver Safety Program

1 (888) 227-7669)

Alzheimer's Association
   <www.alz.org>
   1 (800) 272-3900

American Cancer Society
   <www.cancer.org>
   1 (800) ACS-2345   1 (800) 772-2345

American Diabetes Association
   <www.diabetes.org>
   1 (800) DIABETES   1 (800) 342-2383

American Geriatrics Association (AGS)
   <www.americangeriatrics.org>
   1 (212) 308-1414

American Heart Association
   <www.americanheart.org>
   1 (800) AHA-USA1   1(800) 242-8721

American Lung Association
   <www.lungusa.org>
   1 (800) LUNGUSA   1 (800) 586-4872

American Medical Association (AMA)
   <www.ama-assn.org>
   1 (800) 621-8335
        American Medical Association: Physician's Guide to
        Assessing and Counseling Older Drivers 2005
        1(312) 464-4179

American Stroke Association

    <www.strokeassociation.org>

    1 (888) 4 STROKE   1 (888) 474-7653

The Arthritis Foundation

    <www.arthritis.org>

    1 (800) 568-4045

The Leeza Gibbons Memory Foundation

    <www.memoryfoundation.org>

    1 (888) OK LEEZA   1(888) 655 3392

National Multiple Sclerosis Society

    <nmss.org>

    1 (800) FIGHT MS

    1 (800) 344-4867

National Osteoporosis Foundation

    <www.nor.org>

    1 (202) 223-2226

National Stroke Association

    <www.stroke.org>

    1 (800) STROKES   1 (800) 787-6537

Parkinson's Disease Foundation, Inc.

    <pdf.org>

        Parkinson's Information Service (PINS)

        1 (800) 457-6676

INDEX

97